Virginia
BLUE-RIBBON STREAMS
A Fly-Fishing Guide

HARRY W. MURRAY
Introduction by Lefty Kreh

Virginia
BLUE-RIBBON STREAMS
A Fly-Fishing Guide

HARRY W. MURRAY

Introduction by Lefty Kreh

Frank Amato PORTLAND

Dedication

This book is dedicated to my children:
Milly, Nicki, Liz, Jeff and Susan

Acknowledgments

I am deeply indebted to many people who have helped tremendously in the preparation of this book. Without their assistance it could not be written. They are alphabetically: Tom Blount, Robert Bryant, Bill Burslem, John Coleman, Rhonda Crisman, William Downey, Jerry Fouse, Dennis Hackler, Thomas Hampton, Jeff Handy, John Jessee, Dawn Kirk, Sam Long, Jack McAllister, Larry Mohn, Glenn Morrison, Jeff Murray, Hank Norton, Rusty Painter, Emily Pels, Dick Rabun, Gerald Racey, Ed Resio, L.E. Rhodes Jr., Cindy Simmons, Scott Smith, Harry Steeves, Lee Walker, Charley Waterman, Joe Williams.

Other books by the author

Trout Fishing In The Shenandoah National Park
Fly Fishing For Smallmouth Bass
His Blessing Through Angling

©2000 by Harry W. Murray
ALL RIGHTS RESERVED. No part of this book may be reproduced without the written consent of the publisher, except in the case of brief excerpts in critical reviews and articles.

Published in 2000 by Frank Amato Publications, Inc.
P.O. Box 82112, Portland, Oregon 97282
(503) 653-8108 • www.amatobooks.com

Softbound ISBN: 1-57188-159-X   Hardbound ISBN: 1-57188-200-6
Softbound UPC: 0-66066-00357-7   Hardbound UPC: 0-66066-00414-7

All photographs taken by Harry Murray and Jeff Murray except where noted.

Front Cover Photograph: Chuck Savage
Frontispiece Photograph: Harry W. Murray
Title page photograph: Harry W. Murray
Back Cover Photograph: Chuck Savage
River Maps: Provided by and used with permission of the Virginia Department of Game and Inland Fisheries
Book Design: Tony Amato

Printed in Singapore

3 5 7 9 10 8 6 4

Table of Contents

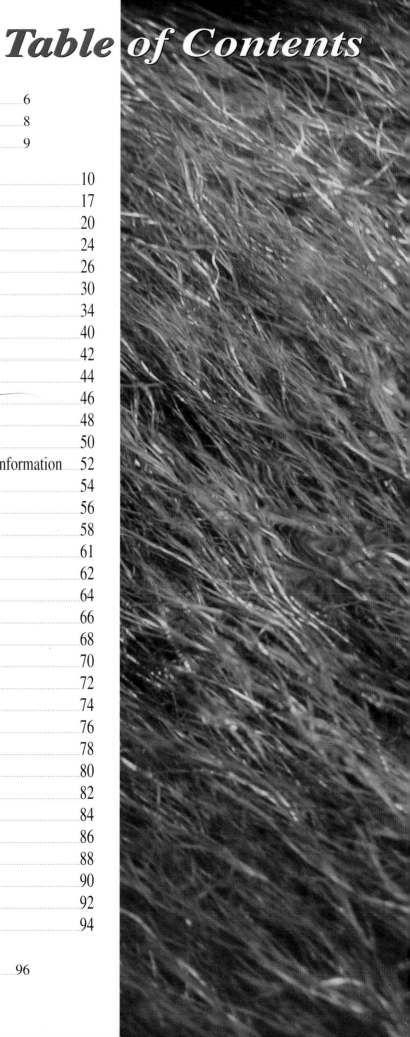

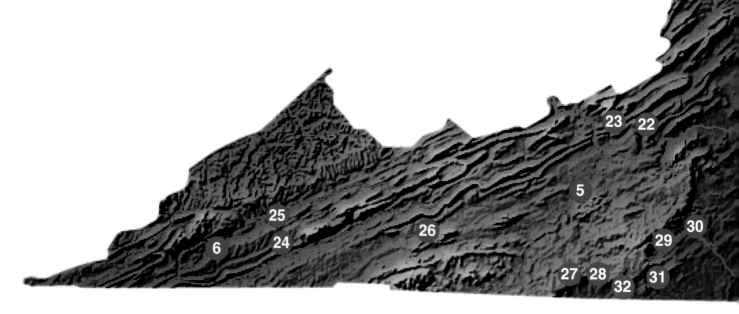

VIRGINIA

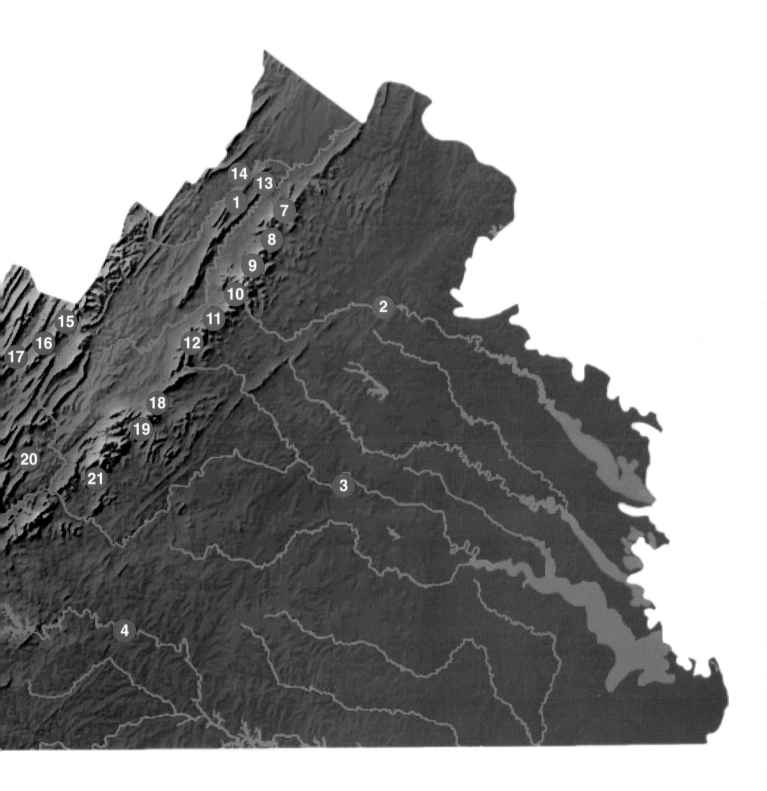

Introduction

In the Mid-Atlantic, from Philadelphia to Richmond, you have dozens of fly fishing clubs and thousands of anglers who enjoy the sport. The state of Virginia offers easy-to-reach fertile fresh waters for all fly fishermen in this area. There is no doubt in my mind that some of the largest river smallmouths in our country live in what is regarded as one of the oldest rivers in the United States—New River in southern Virginia. Drifting its clear waters, I personally have caught smallmouths that were larger than seven pounds.

I would also regard the James River, another Virginia jewel, as perhaps the best river in the East, for its size, for producing smallmouth bass of better than four pounds. The James is easy to wade in most areas and is perfect for fishing from a john boat or canoe. Best of all, it's located near population centers.

The Blue Ridge Mountains pour forth fresh, cold waters that produce some of the cleanest and better trout streams in the East. Wise conservation laws by the state also ensure that trout fishing will do well for the future, too. While the limestone spring streams of south central Pennsylvania have received wide publicity for decades, Virginia sits atop the same type of limestone. And, there are some limestone spring creeks in Virginia that hold wise trout to test the mettle of a fly fisherman.

Harry Murray was born in this fly-fishing heaven. As a kid he roamed the area with his grandfather. Later, he started a fly shop that has become nationally recognized. Harry has fly fished over all of Virginia. He has counseled clients and taught many at his own fly fishing school for years. In short, the man knows where and how to fish Virginia's fresh waters.

He has written this book, which offers all the information you need to fish these waters. Stream by stream, he details the geography of each stream, the type of fish it holds and where and how to fish them. But, Harry also lists motels, bed and breakfast and campground locations. He provides detailed maps of the smallmouth river and complete directions for all of the trout-stream locations. He offers address of canoe and boat rentals, and much more.

If you have any plans for fishing in this state's fresh waters, *Virginia Blue-Ribbon Streams: A Fly-Fishing Guide* by Harry Murray, will fill all your needs.

—Lefty Kreh

Preface

Since Virginia's slogan states that "Virginia Is For Lovers" then *Virginia Blue-Ribbon Streams: A Fly-Fishing Guide* is a book which covers the best streams for lovers of serious angling.

The mountain trout streams are the homes of the beautiful wild brook trout which rise quite aggressively to dry flies. The spring creeks and the tailwater trout streams hold wise old trout that feed selectively on minuscule insects requiring gossamer leaders and tiny dry flies for consistent success. Smallmouth bass in the large rivers may be seen marauding schools of minnows in the shallows in the morning, leaping to grab adult damselflies from the air in the afternoon and sipping spent mayflies from the stream's surface at dusk. Then when one hooks this "gentlemen of the warm water" he puts on a spectacular show with acrobatic jumps that makes us feel privileged just to witness this display.

Many anglers in the Old Dominion sense a blending of fishing with deep history which is just around every turn in the stream. Whether it's the Native American's stalking deer in the heights of Mount Rogers, Daniel Boone floating the Clinch River, the steam locomotive bringing the first smallmouths to the Shenandoah drainage or President Herbert Hoover catching trout in the Blue Ridge Mountains just to "wash his soul", the warmth of the past makes the present more vibrant.

Finally, some anglers feel that fishing the meandering streams in Virginia holds a greater reward than catching the wild fish, greater than sinking into the peaceful solitude of the stream; it is the filling of a previously undetected void with an emotion of complete satisfaction that only God can give.

Chapter 1
Shenandoah River

The Shenandoah River is my home water. I was born, raised and still live practically on the bank of the North Fork of the Shenandoah River in Edinburg. In fact, my office window in my fly shop overlooks one of the best pools in Stoney Creek, a feeder stream to the North Fork which it joins just a mile downstream.

My aging almost-blind grandfather loved fishing and started taking me along when I was five years old. Grandfather used pretty good tackle, but I relegated to using a sawed-off broom handle with very heavy black nylon braided line. However, I can still remember my first fish and the exact spot that I caught it. The fish was a tiny rock bass and we were fishing below the tail race of the Edinburg grain mill which was one block from our home.

Grandfather established a reputation as a skillful fisherman in his early years by catching a five-pound fourteen-ounce smallmouth bass on the North Fork of the Shenandoah River at Red Banks in 1914. He knew the Pitman boys who lived in the Red Banks Mansion, and I'm sure he was proud of the fact that all ten of them served in the Confederate Army. However, a certain railroad trip that took place less than ten years before the boys went to war was more meaningful to him, for this was how the seed of his bass came to Virginia.

Originally there were no smallmouth bass in the eastern watersheds in Virginia. But in 1854 Mr. William Shriver of Wheeling, West Virginia solicited the help of Mr. A. G. Stabler, a conductor on the Baltimore and Ohio Railroad, to help him move thirty smallmouth bass to the east. The bass were carefully removed from Wheeling Creek, where they occurred naturally, and placed in a large perforated tin bucket made to fit the water tank of the locomotive. At each regular water station between Wheeling and Cumberland, Maryland fresh water was added. Arriving at their new home in excellent condition, Mr. Shriver placed the bass in the basin of the Chesapeake and Ohio Canal, from which they had free egress and ingress to the Potomac River.

From this meager start the bass spread quickly up the Potomac River and its feeder river the Shenandoah. By 1865 there were confirmed reports of excellent smallmouth fishing far up the Shenandoah drainage.

The North Fork of the Shenandoah River has many riffles that hold a great population of smallmouth bass.

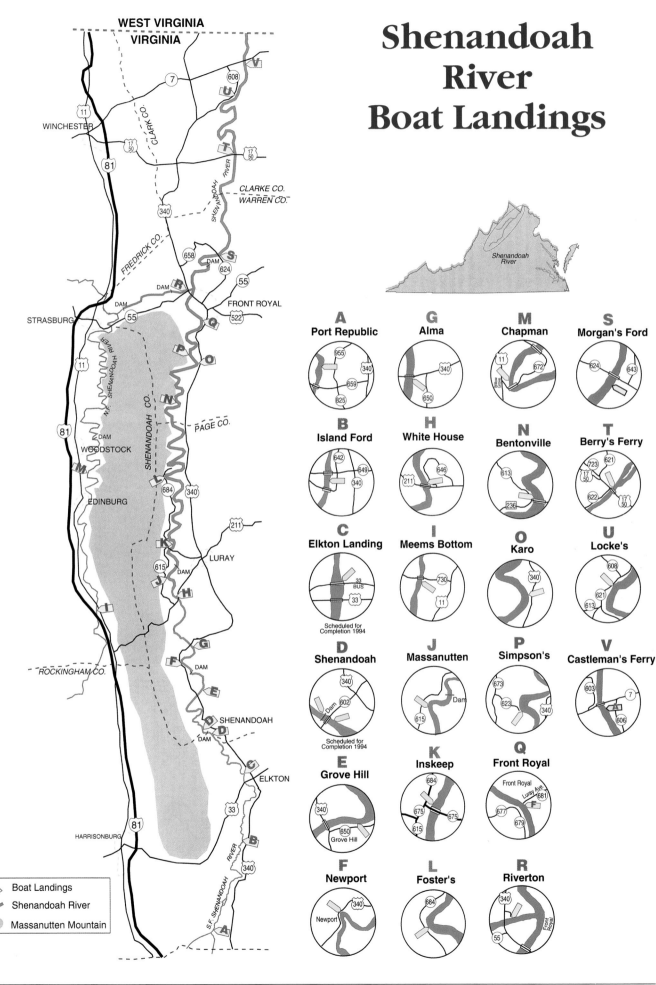

Shenandoah River Boat Landings

A Port Republic

B Island Ford

C Elkton Landing
Scheduled for Completion 1994

D Shenandoah
Scheduled for Completion 1994

E Grove Hill

F Newport

G Alma

H White House

I Meems Bottom

J Massanutten

K Inskeep

L Foster's

M Chapman

N Bentonville

O Karo

P Simpson's

Q Front Royal

R Riverton

S Morgan's Ford

T Berry's Ferry

U Locke's

V Castleman's Ferry

Legend:
- Boat Landings
- Shenandoah River
- Massanutten Mountain

Various state and federal agencies as well as other private individuals were instrumental in spreading the smallmouths throughout Virginia from this point on, but anglers today as well as in Grandfather's day owe a great deal to Mr. Shriver's initial efforts.

The Shenandoah Drainage

The North Fork, South Fork and main stem of the Shenandoah River provide about 150 miles of exciting smallmouth fishing.

The North Fork of the Shenandoah River begins in the rugged Allegheny Mountains west of New Market and flows northeast through the Shenandoah Valley. The South Fork begins in the vicinity of the town of Port Republic where the North, Middle and South rivers join. It skirts the foothills of the Blue Ridge Mountains as it flows north to meet the North Fork at Front Royal. The main stem of the Shenandoah River then flows north through Virginia's beautiful horse farm country to empty into the Potomac River at Harpers Ferry.

Fishing the River

One of the greatest factors governing angling success is being able to fish in the right water level at the right time, and the physical makeup of the Shenandoah drainage simplifies this task greatly.

Let me show you how I play this water level game and maybe it will help you.

The North Fork contains only about one fifth of the water volume of the South Fork, and by mid-May the North Fork is at a good fishable level.

Partly for nostalgic reasons and partly because of the quality of the fishing, for the past twenty years I've been starting the season on a stretch of the North Fork close to Edinburg. The beautiful pools and churning riffles here remind me of the Gallatin River just above the Gallatin Gateway in Montana.

As a youngster I used to seine this area to catch bait to sell and use so I know it is loaded with sculpin minnows and hellgrammites (the larva of the dobson fly). I'm a firm believer in matching my flies to the natural foods in each area so Ed Shenk's Sculpin in sizes 4 and 6 and Murray's Hellgrammite in sizes 4 and 6 are the main flies I use here when the stream is full in the beginning of the season.

By early June that section of the North Fork downstream from Edinburg is usually in good shape and I do most of my fishing here as well as conducting my smallmouth fly-fishing schools here. There are many sections in the stretch of the North Fork around Woodstock and Toms Brook that have great populations of chub minnows and Shenk's White Streamer in sizes 4 and 6 and the Pearl Marauder in sizes 6 and 8 are extremely effective.

The South Fork and the main stem of the Shenandoah are usually at a good fishable level by mid-June. Although these are both larger rivers, lending themselves well to float fishing with canoes, most smallmouth fly anglers prefer doing their serious fishing by wading and use the canoes simply as a means to get from one hot spot to the next.

This is the time of the year many anglers go to surface bugs on all three rivers with great success. Popping bugs and deer-hair bugs both in sizes 4, 6 and 8 and dry flies in sizes 6, 8, and 10 are all very effective. My favorites here are the Shenandoah Blue Popper, the Tapply Hair Bug in green/white and Improved Sofa Pillow.

During July and August all three rivers fish well unless we have a year of below normal rainfall, rendering the North Fork too low, in which case we spend our time on the South Fork and main stem.

This is one of my favorite times to fish the Shenandoah because nymphs, streamers, surface bugs and drys are all very productive, and I can fish with the flies I enjoy for the type water I'm on. By July the aquatic grass beds have developed enough to provide a good habitat for the nymphs and minnows. The smallmouths are very much aware of this smorgasbord and move in to feed aggressively. If I could pick only one area for all my smallmouth fishing it would be around the aquatic grass beds. They seldom let me down!

If the depth of the stream in and around the grass beds is from two to three feet deep and the current is moving at a slow to moderate rate I do well by fishing surface bugs along the edges of the grass and in the small open bays that often exist within the grass beds. If, on the other hand, the water adjacent to the grass beds is more than three feet deep or moving at a fast rate, I get my best results by fishing a nymph or a streamer along the stream bottom. Whitlock's Damselfly Nymph, the Silver Outcast Streamer and the Olive Strymphs are all very productive for me along the grass beds.

Throughout the summer and into mid-September we often find the smallmouths feeding on the surface on a variety of natural insects and do well with dry flies. The most prevalent natural is the damselfly which we see by the thousands all about the rivers, but a broad variety of mayflies, caddisflies and terrestrial insects are also available to the bass.

September is an excellent time to fish the Shenandoah and until the latter part of the month you can take the bass with streamers, nymphs and on the surface. However, by the end of September or early October the bass commence a mini-migration into the deeper pockets and pools. Most of these areas are less than six feet deep so we can still fish them effectively with our flies.

Using a Scientific Anglers Sinking-tip III line and the Lead Eye Hellgrammites or a Murray's Madtom I do quite well until the middle or latter part of October. After this the water temperature drops so low that the smallmouths do not feed actively.

Most smallmouth anglers prefer 9-foot rods which balance with size 7 or 8 lines. Basic single-action reels which will hold these line sizes with fifty yards of backing are popular. I like 9-foot compound knotted leaders which taper down to 2X or 3X for most of my bass fishing. Floating weight-forward bass bug tapered lines cover most of our needs. However, early in the season when the streams are high and late in the fall when the bass are in the deepest water, a moderately fast sinking-tip line with a 6-foot leader is best.

Floating the River

In order for you to find good fishing on the North and South Fork's and main stem of the Shenandoah River let's set up some imaginary float trips so you can see the access points and different types of water. As well as launching a canoe at these points most provide excellent fishing by just wading. However, keep in mind that the land around these access points is privately owned and is not open to the public. You can enter and leave the river only at the public access sites.

Floating and Fishing the North Fork of the Shenandoah River

You can launch your canoe at the game commission access site at Meems Bottom (I) off Route 730 just a hundred yards off Route 11. The next legal take-out is about 10 miles downstream at the end of Route 695 east of Edinburg. This take-out spot is only suitable for canoes and small boats. This is a long float unless you have a very full stream so plan your time accordingly.

The next float downstream is to launch at the end of Route 695 below the old washed-out bridge east of Edinburg and take-out at the mouth of Stoney Creek along Route 760 east of Edinburg about three miles downstream. You can actually launch at the mouth of Stoney Creek and fish the deep water above the Edinburg Dam which is excellent for smallmouths and sunfish, but if you drift as far down as the dam you must paddle back upstream and take-out at your launch site because it is illegal to portage this dam. The dam is only about a mile downstream from the launch site and the paddling is very easy, so don't pass this one up because the fishing is excellent. Both the launch and take-out spots are suitable for small boats and canoes.

The next launch site is Chapman's Landing (M) on Route 672 just off Route 11, two miles north of Edinburg. This is excellent water for smallmouths and panfish in every type water you could hope for: deep runs, fast riffles, and deep pools are all found in the three-mile stretch down to the dam three miles north. There are many large largemouth bass in the

The smallmouth bass in the Shenandoah River take a broad variety of flies.

deep water above Chapman's Dam. It is not legal or safe to portage this dam, but it is easy to paddle back up to Chapman's Landing.

There is good water to wade above and below the Route 609 bridge off Route 670 two miles east of Woodstock. However, this is not a legal launch site for canoes unless you

Several old power dams on the North Fork of the Shenandoah River add to the variety of the action.

want to paddle back and take-out at the same spot.

You can launch a canoe or wade the water below Burnshire Bridge by parking on the downstream side of the bridge on Route 758 two miles west of Woodstock off Route 11 and Route 665.

The take-out point is at the Route 663 bridge about one mile off Route 11 north of Woodstock. The upper portion of this five-mile float has many great riffles where the Murray's Hellgrammites will give you many nice smallmouths. The lower one-third of this float takes you into the backed-up water from the old deteriorating Stonewall Dam where one can do well by fishing the shaded banks with hair bugs and poppers.

The next access point is along the upper area where Route 661 parallels the river. There is excellent fishing here by wading with many riffles and pools, but there is no area to take a canoe out downstream, so save this for wading. There is also private land along the lower reaches of Route 661 so respect this area.

Floating and Fishing the South Fork of the Shenandoah River

By launching at Port Republic (A) off Route 955 you have excellent smallmouth water for ten miles down to Island Ford (B). The deep water on the right side of the island about one mile downstream is worth working thoroughly with nymphs and streamers for there are some large bass here. Portage the old power dam above Island Ford on the left. Take-out on the right side of the river between the bridges along Route 642.

Between Island Ford (B) and Elkton (C) you have a great seven-mile float. The mixture of deep pools and fast riffles here offer a variety of smallmouth actions. Take-out on the right side of the river near the second Route 33 bridge.

From Elkton (C) to Shenandoah (D) is a seven mile float. The upper area of this float provides smallmouths, sunfish and rock bass, but as you approach the dam at Shenandoah you may pick up largemouths and musky. Take out above the dam on the right side of the river at Route 602.

Launching below the dam at Shenandoah (D) and floating to Grove Hill (E) gives you eight miles with all water types and fish. Save time in this float to beach your canoe and carefully wade and fish the water from the Route 340 bridge to the take-out point on the right on Route 650. This is beautiful smallmouth water with many ledges and deep cuts.

The river between Grove Hill (E) and Newport (F) covers six miles with several deep flat areas. Fish here are very wary in low-water periods so approach them very carefully. In addition to the smallmouths in the fast water you will find largemouths and musky in the deep slow areas. Take out on the left below the riffle at Newport along Route 340. Both of these access points are best suited for canoes and small boats.

From Newport (F) to Alma (G) is a popular three-mile float with many riffles and runs. One can easily devote a full day to this area by wading the best water after beaching the canoe. The take-out on the right side of the river above the Route 340 bridge is not suitable for trailers.

The float from Alma (G) to White House (H) covers seven miles of good smallmouth water with a great variety of water types. I've done well here by fishing the western (left) bank

through much of this water with surface bug from mid-afternoon until dusk. Many great grass beds form here in July. The take-out is under the 211 bridge on the right.

Putting in at the White House Bridge (H) and floating to the Massanutten Landing (J) gives you four miles of mostly deep water backed up by an old mill dam in the upper area and a small power dam in the lower area. The area around the Massanutten Landing on the left bank is popular for largemouth bass and is good all the way downstream to the dam.

I would not recommend launching at the Massanutten site and plan to take-out at the Inskeep site. There is a dangerous dam in the middle that is not easy to portage and there is only about three miles of river anyway.

The float from Inskeeper (K) on the left side of the river below the Route 675 bridge to Foster's Landing (L) takes you through nine miles of some of the most productive smallmouth bass water in the state. Here you'll find riffles, pools, ledges and lush aquatic grass beds with bass which will take a broad variety of bugs, nymphs and streamers. The Murray's Madtom is very productive in this area as is the Shenandoah Damsel Popper. Foster's Landing is on the left side of the river along Route 684.

Taking smallmouth bass on the surface is a special thrill on the South Fork of the Shenandoah River.

From Foster's Landing (L) to Bentonville (N) covers 18 miles. The water continues much like the water above Foster's in the upper reaches but it slows in some areas close to Bentonville. The smallmouth action here is excellent and be sure to take your camera for there are mountain ranges on both sides of the river making this one of the most beautiful stretches of river in the state. There are numerous campgrounds and National Forest access points for wading and floating in this stretch. Since the access and regulations may vary from year to year you may want to stop by or call Murray's Fly Shop in Edinburg for current information (540/984-4212). The take-out point is downstream of the bridge on Route 613.

From Bentonville (N) you can float about nine miles down to Karo (O) or continue another half mile and take-out at Simpson's (P). This is all good smallmouth water and I like to allow time to wade and fish the many ledge pockets and grass beds. There is a very productive large riffle a short distance below Karo which is well worth fishing thoroughly with streamers and nymphs. The Karo take-out is on the right just off Route 340. The Simpson's take-out is on the left on Route 623 off Route 673.

You can launch at Simpson's (P) and float six miles down to Front Royal (Q). Much of this can be easily waded which is the way I prefer to fish the numerous grass beds which are found here late in the summer. The take-out point is on the right just upstream of Route 681.

The four-mile float from Front Royal (Q) to Riverton (R) is your last shot at the Forks of the Shenandoah River and it is excellent water. The upper part of this area is shallow enough to provide excellent surface fishing with hair bugs and poppers while the last part is deeper and produces well with streamers and nymphs in the deep pools as well as surface bugs along the banks and grass beds. Take out one-quarter mile upstream on the North Fork at the Riverton Landing off Route 340.

The cuts between the ledges along the aquatic grass beds hold many large smallmouths.

Floating and Fishing the Main Stem of the Shenandoah River

By launching at Riverton (R) and floating the thirteen miles down to Morgan's Ford (S) on the main Shenandoah you have an excellent chance to get fine action for both smallmouths and largemouths. Good smallmouth fishing is found in the upper part of this float, then you start picking up largemouth in the slow water above the dam four miles downstream. Portage the dam and you are back into smallmouths. The take-out is by the Route 624 bridge on the right.

Floating from Morgan's Ford (S) to Berry's Ferry (T) takes you through eleven miles of very diverse water types all of which have good populations of smallmouths. Early in the season some anglers find that the use of fast sinking-tip fly lines helps run their nymphs and streamers through the deep runs in this area. The dense aquatic grass beds which form here late in the season provide excellent bass cover and surface bug action. Take out on the left side of the river under the Route 50 bridge.

The float from Berry's Ferry (T) down ten miles to Lockes (U) takes you through some special water. For one thing you'll

The main Shenandoah River is one of the most productive streams in Virginia, holding great numbers of smallmouths, largemouths and sunfish.

Smallmouths grow well on the abundance of foods in the Shenandoah River and will take large streamers and surface bugs.

see the remains of old Indian fish traps. I always devote extra time to fishing these traps for the smallmouth action can be outstanding immediately above and below them. Also my mind often drifts back to try to imagine the activities that must have gone on here before settlers moved in. The meandering nature of this stretch of river and the mixed gradient afford a variety of water from which we simply select the areas we like best and that fish well. Take out at Lockes on Route 621 on the left side of the river. These are both excellent boat ramps allowing the launching of trailered boats.

The last float is from Lockes (U) to Castleman's Ferry (V). This covers five miles of beautiful water laced with riffles and islands. I often get some of my best smallmouth action around the islands, for they enable me to take advantage of various water levels. Consider heavily weighted streamers and nymphs below the heavy runs in late May and June. Late in the summer the aquatic grass beds give us great surface action. Take out on the right side at the Route 7 bridge. These are both excellent boat ramps permitting the use of trailered boats.

As you can see the Shenandoah drainage provides a vast amount of angling. One needs simply to find what he likes.

Activities and Services

The Shenandoah Valley provides many rewarding activities for the angler and the family.

There is a wealth of interesting history on the American Civil War with almost each town and city having their own museum. The battlefield and museum at New Market where the VMI cadets fought so valiantly is especially well done.

The mountains along the sides of the valley contain some of Virginia's best trout streams. Many of the streams in Shenandoah National Park and the George Washington

National Forest actually drain into the Shenandoah River. These are all covered separately in the chapters on trout streams.

Floating, fishing and camping along the river is possible on the South Fork of the Shenandoah River due to the abundance of George Washington National Forest land adjacent to the river. Information on maps showing these areas is available under "Maps" at the end of this chapter.

FACILITIES

BED & BREAKFAST:
The Inn at Narrow Passage
U.S. 11 South
P.O. Box 608
Woodstock, VA 22664
Phone: (540) 459-8000 or
1-800-459-8002
http://www.innatnarrowpassage.com

The Edinburg Inn
218 South Main Street
Edinburg, VA 22824
Phone: (540) 984-8286

The Woodward House on Manor Grade Bed & Breakfast
413 S. Royal Ave.
Front Royal, VA 22630
Phone: (540) 635-7010 &
1-800-635-7011

MOTELS:
Budget Host
1290 South Main Street
Woodstock, VA 22664
Phone: (540) 459-4086

Ramada Inn
P.O. Box 44 (Exit 283, I-81)
Woodstock, VA 22664
Phone: (540) 459-5000 or
1-800-272-6232

Quality Inn Skyline Drive
10 Commerce Ave.
Front Royal, VA 22630
Phone: (540) 635-3161 or
1-800-821-4488

Front Royal Motel
1400 Shenandoah Ave.
Front Royal, VA 22630
Phone: (540) 635-4114

CAMPGROUNDS:
Creekside Campground
108 Palmyra Rd.
P.O. Box 277
Edinburg, VA 22824
Phone: (540) 984-4299

National Forest Campgrounds
Lee Ranger District
109 Molineu Rd.
Edinburg, VA 22824
Phone: (540) 984-4101

Front Royal KOA
P.O. Box 274
Front Royal, VA 22630 Phone:
(540) 635-2741 or
1-800-KOA-9114

MAPS:
Shenandoah Publishing Company
121 Main Street
P.O. Box 156
Edinburg, VA 22824
Phone: (540) 984-4212

CANOE RENTALS:
Shenandoah River Outfitters
6502 S. Page Valley Rd.
Luray, VA 22835
Phone: (540) 743-4159

Downriver Canoe Co.
P.O. Box 10
884 Indian Hollow Rd.
Bentonville, VA 22610
Phone: (540) 635-5526 or
1-800-338-1963

Front Royal Canoe Co.
P.O. Box 473
Front Royal, VA 22630
Phone: (540) 635-5440 or
1-800-270-8808

GUIDE SERVICE & SCHOOLS:
Murray's Fly Shop
121 Main St.
P.O. Box 156
Edinburg, VA 22824
Phone: (540) 984-4212
Fax (540) 984-4895
e-mail murrays@shentel.net
www.murraysflyshop.com

CHAMBER OF COMMERCE:
Shenandoah Valley Travel Association
P.O. Box 1040
277 W. Old Cross Rd.
New Market, VA 22844
Phone: (540) 740-3132
Fax: (540) 740-3100
E-mail: svta@shentel.net

Chapter 2
Rappahannock/Rapidan River

These sister rivers gain their origins from the cool hollows high on the eastern slopes of the Blue Ridge Mountains. They meander through the rich farmland in the Piedmont area of Virginia then join east of the historic Chancellorsville Civil War Battlefield to flow through the city of Fredricksburg where they receive their first taste of salt water.

This combined journey provides anglers with about 140 miles of excellent fishing for smallmouth bass, redbreast sunfish, and bluegills and in April there are great runs of striped bass and shad.

Good fishing begins in May and lasts until October, one needs to adapt his tactics to the level of the streams as dictated by the run-off and the gradient of the rivers.

In many years the full water levels in May call for fishing nymphs and streamers slowly along the stream bottom. If the particular run or pool you are fishing is not exceedingly fast this can often be achieved with a floating fly line by simply adding split shot above the fly or by incorporating six to twenty inches of miniature lead head in the leader.

Some of the most productive flies on these two rivers early in the season are Shenk's White Streamer, Black and Olive Strymphs, Clouser's Deep Sculpin and Murray's Hellgrammites all in sizes 4 and 6.

As these streams drop in June and July deer-hair surface bugs, poppers and big dry flies become very effective. The aquatic grass beds usually develop well at this time and great surface smallmouth fishing can be found along the edges of the grass and in the open bays which form within them.

Many anglers find that by mixing their tactics throughout the summer they get the best results.

For example, if you are floating the river in a canoe and come to a high-gradient section with many ledges and boulders

The Rappahannock River is a fine smallmouth river. The "rock garden" above Kelly's Ford is an excellent stretch.

scattered throughout fairly fast water you may want to beach your canoe and thoroughly fish each deep run and pocket with a nymph or streamer. Whereas, if you spot a heavily shaded bank where the water is three feet deep, flowing at a moderate pace over a cobblestone bottom, it might be wise to fish this area thoroughly with surface bugs.

If you happen to fish this area late in the summer during a low-water year you might find that the Rappahannock River gives you better action than the Rapidan River since it carries about a third more water. This, of course, can help us keep from spooking the fish.

Also, a ploy which has worked well for me on the Rappahannock River late in August when the water level is low is to fish the ledge and grass bed areas upstream with poppers and hair bugs. During the middle of the day this is most effective in the shaded areas, but once the sun gets low on the horizon you can take bass all across the river on the surface.

In order for you to experience good fishing on these rivers let's set up an imaginary float trip which will show you the access points, areas where you can camp and a few special tactics to use along the way.

For the angler who likes a fairly short float trip which allows him time to beach the canoe and carefully explore the best-looking water by wading, the uppermost float trip on the Rappahannock River is ideal. You can launch your canoe at the

Smallmouths feed aggressively on adult damselflies by leaping into the air to grab them.

old U.S. Highway 29 bridge in Remington and float 4.5 miles to the Kelly's Ford access site.

About three miles downstream from Remington begins the "rock garden" which is sometimes referred to more formally as the Kelly's Ford Rapids. Regardless of the name one cares to

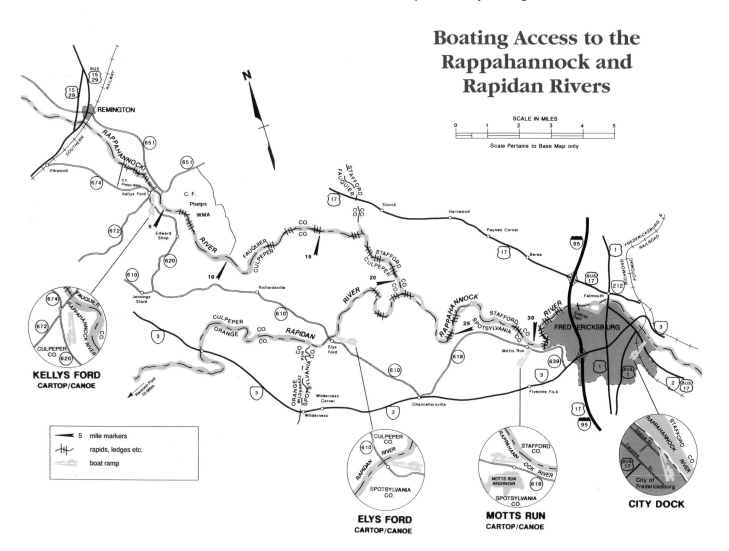

Boating Access to the Rappahannock and Rapidan Rivers

put on this section it is ideal smallmouth bass water. You can fish it across and downstream with streamers or upstream dead drift with nymphs or work the grass beds with surface bugs. I've had some of my best fishing in this stretch.

This stretch contains part of the Virginia Department of Game and Inland Fisheries 4,500-acre C.F. Phelps Wildlife Management Area. This is an ideal area for camping or a streamside lunch.

When launching at Kelly's Fork access site you have a 25-mile float to the next take-out point which is at Motts Run access point off Route 618. There is about six miles of the C.F. Phelps Wildlife Management area just below Kelly's Ford on the left side as you float downstream which is available for camping. Also, the city of Fredricksburg has numerous tracts of land along the river totaling 4,800 acres. Camping is permitted on part of this land. For specific information on this land you can contact the city of Fredricksburg at 540/372-1023.

The first several miles of this float trip takes you through long flat pools with few riffles. Some anglers like to fish these banks with streamers and poppers while their partner paddles the canoe carefully to put them on the best bank and keep them the proper casting distance off the bank.

Next you will float into a section of the river with steep, rocky bluffs and heavy timber. There are more riffles here offering a broader variety of fishing, and the action is usually quite good.

As you approach the confluence where the Rapidan River enters from the southwest you will find outstanding smallmouth water. There are numerous strong riffles and rapids here which provide perfect habitats for sculpin minnows and hellgrammites. During the early part of the season when the river is flowing at a full, but fishable, pace you may want to use a fast sinking-tip fly line with a six-foot leader to successfully fish your flies in the deep, fast pools and runs.

Below the confluence of the Rapidan River the gradient slows again and you'll see numerous riffles which are actually the remains of old dams. The Rapidan River increases the water volume of this part of the Rappahannock River about one-third.

There is excellent fishing for smallmouth bass in this part of the river during the summer around the aquatic grass beds. The abundance of minnows and aquatic insects around these grass beds attract the bass and they feed heavily on both along the edges and throughout the open water within the grassy areas.

My personal preference is to fish these grass beds with deer-hair surface bugs and poppers. However, if the water adjacent to the grass is three to four feet deep or if the current is forceful I often go to streamers such as the Silver Outcast or Shenk's White Streamer.

If you would like to take advantage of some fast-flowing water as well as flat tidal water you can launch your canoe at the Motts Run access point and float to the Fredricksburg City Dock about three miles downstream.

It is necessary to portage around the Embrey Dam on the left side of the river as you are floating downstream. As you approach the fall line above the U.S. Highway 1 Bridge it is best to stay to the left side of the river since there is some dangerous fast water on the right side. Below the Route 1 Bridge the river slows greatly and there is some good fishing here for largemouth bass and black crappie.

The Rapidan River

This is a fine smallmouth river, and many knowledgeable anglers like to take advantage of it in the spring if the Rappahannock River is a little high. In fact, throughout the season it is quite likely that one of these rivers will be clear and fish well when the other one is discolored since they drain different watersheds. Carrying only about two-thirds the volume of its sister river, the Rapidan is a little easier to wade and fish. However, late in the summer the Rapidan is usually much lower than the Rappahannock so most anglers prefer the latter at that time.

You can access the Rapidan River at Raccoon Ford at Route 611 off Route 522 for wading. However, if you are planning to float from here down to Ely's Ford downstream of the Route 610 bridge you will be covering 19 miles of the river which is a long float for one day. The river flows through private land here so be sure to gain the permission of any landowner beforehand if you plan to camp and spend the night. This section flows through a mixture of farm land and remote country and thus receives little angling pressure. There is a good action here during June and early July by fishing the shaded banks with poppers and deer-hair surface bugs as you float along.

If you are interested in American Civil War history many significant events took place in this whole area. In fact, General J.E.B. Stuart was close by Ely's Ford when he received word that General Stonewall Jackson had been seriously wounded in the battle at Chancellorsville, just to the south, and that he would be required to take command of this portion of General R. E. Lee's army.

The float from Ely's Ford on the Rapidan down sixteen miles to Motts Run access point on the Rappahannock River is one of the most productive and scenic in the area.

The gradient of the river increases nicely a short distance below Ely's Ford and many anglers like to park here and just wade this water and not use a canoe. Throughout the summer one can expect good smallmouth action here with surface bugs unless the river gets very low.

There is about eight miles of good water down to the confluence with the Rappahannock with some of the best smallmouth water occurring in the last mile. The drop here is very

The fast stretches of the Rapidan River hold the best populations of smallmouth bass.

A fringe benefit on the Rapidan River is the great numbers of sunfish you catch throughout its length.

rapid and there is a great amount of minnow and insect life available for the bass. Streamers, nymphs and surface bugs are all very productive in this section.

Once you reach the confluence with the Rappahannock River your take-out point at Mott's Run is about eight miles downstream.

Practically all of these access points provide good fishing by wading if you prefer not to use a canoe. However, remember where there is privately owned land along the banks so one must stay in the river. Often when I plan to wade I'll go in at an access site and fish nymphs and surface bugs up one side of the river for half the time I plan to fish then turn and fish streamers back down the other side to the access site. On the lower reaches of our largest rivers one can wade and fish all day taking dozens of large smallmouths without getting out of sight of the access site. I've often done this with great success when guiding anglers who prefer not to float the rivers.

Chapter 3
James River

The James River offers the angler some of the finest small-mouth fishing in the country. For 212 miles from Eagle Rock to Richmond you can fish your way from the foothills of the Allegheny Mountains, slice through the beautiful Blue Ridge Mountains then glide into the rolling Piedmont country. You can pick up smallmouths and sunfish all the way and if you hook something you cannot hold that finally breaks you off you have just met the resident musky of the James River.

In order for you to plan your trip to the James River let's first examine some of the effective tactics and fly patterns, then we'll explore its high points as if we were going to float its full length, and finally we'll list some facilities for canoe rental and lodging.

Good fishing usually starts in late May. Even in its upper reaches the James is a big river and it carries a large water volume. Many anglers find that they make some of their best catches early in the season with deep-running flies such as Clousers Deep Sculpins and Murray's Hellgrammites. Fast sinking-tip fly lines are often a great help in fishing these flies along the bottoms of the deep pools and powerful runs. In order to take the greatest advantage of these lines I like to use a 6-foot leader tapered down to 1X.

Surface bugs come into their own by mid-June with Whitlock's Deer Hair Bugs, the Potomac Popper and the Shenandoah Sliders all in sizes 4 and 6 producing well. On some occasions these actually take more smallmouths for me than the nymphs and streamers. For example, in a recent school I conducted on the James River all of the anglers dredged the depths with every bottom-running fly we could think of, fished with every tactic possible, but we didn't take the numbers of bass I felt we should. By moving many of the students in against the banks and switching over to surface bugs we got some great action.

Now, I'm not saying we should neglect the deep pools and weighted flies. However, I encourage you to keep an open mind and experiment with both ploys well into fall.

Once the water starts cooling in late September one usually does best by working the depths again.

The James River is one of the largest smallmouth rivers in the country affording great fishing and an abundance of public access areas.

FACILITIES

CANOE RENTALS:
Clore Bros. Outfitters
5927 River Rd.
Fredricksburg, VA 22407
Phone: (540) 786-7749 or
1-800-704-7749

CAMPGROUNDS:
Fredricksburg KOA
7400 Brookside Lane
Fredricksburg, VA 22408
Phone: (540) 898-7252 or
1-800-562-1889

Aquia Pine Campground
3071 Jefferson Davis Hwy.
Stafford, VA 22554
Phone: (540) 659-3447

BED & BREAKFAST:
Fredricksburg Colonial Inn
1707 Princess Ann St.
Fredricksburg, VA 22401
Phone: (540) 371-5666

Braehead Bed & Breakfast
123 Lee Dr.
Fredricksburg, VA 22401
Phone: (540) 899-3648

MOTELS/HOTELS:
Sheraton Inn
2801 Plank Rd.
Fredricksburg, VA 22401
Phone: (540) 786-8321 or
1-800-682-1049

Ramada Inn
2802 Plank Rd.
Fredricksburg, VA 22401
Phone: (540) 786-8361 or
1-800-2RAMADA

GENERAL INFORMATION:
Fredricksburg Information Center
706 Caroline St.
Fredricksburg VA 22401
1-800-678-4748

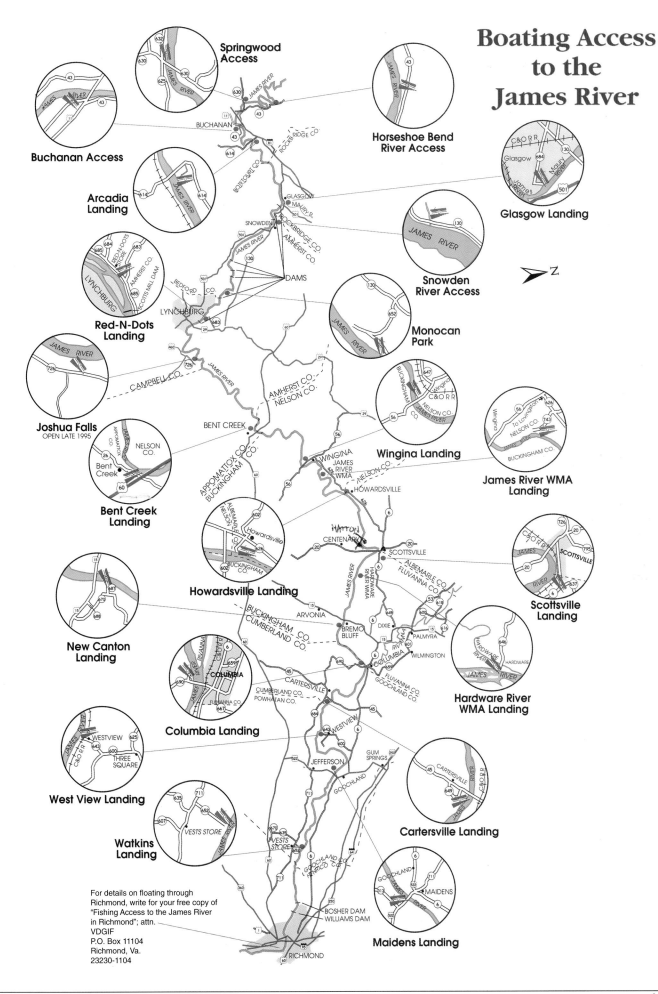

Boating Access to the James River

Buchanan Access

Springwood Access

Horseshoe Bend River Access

Glasgow Landing

Arcadia Landing

Red-N-Dots Landing

Snowden River Access

Monocan Park

Joshua Falls
OPEN LATE 1995

Bent Creek Landing

Wingina Landing

James River WMA Landing

New Canton Landing

Howardsville Landing

Scottsville Landing

Hardware River WMA Landing

West View Landing

Columbia Landing

Watkins Landing

Cartersville Landing

Maidens Landing

For details on floating through Richmond, write for your free copy of "Fishing Access to the James River in Richmond"; attn. VDGIF P.O. Box 11104 Richmond, Va. 23230-1104

Floating the James River

Just upstream of the town of Buchanan the Horseshoe Bend access point is located on Route 43. You have a 2.8-mile float downstream to the Springwood access on the right side of the river along Route 632. There are many great areas to wade and fish the riffles and runs here so many anglers use the canoe primarily to get from one hotspot to the next.

From Springwood to Buchanan is a 3.6-mile float with more strong riffles and runs punctuated with deep pools. This is ideal smallmouth water and I've done very well here late in the summer by fishing the dense grass beds along the banks with the Shenandoah Slider Bugs and Tapply Hair Bugs. The deep pools produce well with a Shenk's White Streamer. The take-out is on the right side of the river just upstream of the Route 11 bridge.

From Buchanan down to Arcadia you have five miles of stream with a broad variety of cover and stream depths. The deep cuts between the ledges can produce some large bass to nymphs and streamers, and there are some powerful muskies here. The Arcadia access site is on the left side of the river just below the Route 614 bridge.

The float from Arcadia to Glasgow covers 12.6 miles. There are many areas here where one can get outstanding surface-bug fishing tight to the right banks, especially in the last several hours of the day. Allow time to fish where the Maury River enters the James from the left. This area is loaded with food and it gave me one of the largest smallmouths I've ever caught. Take out on the left bank along Route 684 just up the Maury.

The float from Glasgow down to Snowden takes you through three miles of some of the most beautiful scenery and finest smallmouth fishing in the state. There are many great rapids in the Gorge where you will get outstanding action with nymphs and streamers. The water below Balcony Falls is especially productive so allow several hours to cover this well. The take-out is on the left bank along Route 130 just downstream of the railroad bridge. The dam below Snowden prevents floating downstream from here.

The Monocan Park access point near Elon at the end of Route 652 gives you good access to the deep water above the Reusens Dam. Some of the best fishing in the several miles of flat water here is by working the banks with poppers and the deep water with nymphs and streamers. If the water is cold you may want to try the underwater flies with a sinking-tip fly line.

By launching your canoe at the Red-N-Dots Market private ramp (fee required) you have access to the excellent deep flat water above Scott's Mill Dam. This is interesting and productive water to fish because of the varying character of the water around these islands. By fishing the shaded sides tight to the islands with surface bugs you can consistently take large-mouths, smallmouths and sunfish. Many anglers play this game

A selection of streamers which match the natural foods on the James River is good insurance for taking the largest smallmouths consistently.

right up to when it is completely dark because it is very productive and the take-out is easy.

The float from Joshua Falls to Bent Creek covers 15 miles of excellent water for fly fishing for smallmouths. Much of this is easily waded so allow time to beach your canoe and carefully fish the riffles and cuts between the ledges. Put-in along Route 726 near the Campbell County line on the west side of the river and take-out on the right side of the river along Route 26 upstream of the Route 60 bridge.

Floating from Bent Creek to Wingina covers 12.4 miles. This area is equally productive by wading and floating and the most effective anglers use both methods. Be sure to allow time to fish the rich riffles in this float with nymphs and streamers. Take out on the left side of the river just upstream of the Route 56 bridge.

The Wingina to James River Wildlife Management area is 2.2 miles of fairly shallow water. Late in the summer one can find excellent smallmouth fishing with surface bugs around the aquatic grass beds late in the evenings. Take out on the left bank at the end of Route 743.

The James River WMA to Howardsville float is 8.6 miles with some excellent smallmouth action around the islands and the shallow riffles. The take-out point is off Route 626 at the mouth of Rockfish River.

From Howardsville to Scottsville is a 9.8-mile float. Since Scottsville is the center of the fishing in this area this is a very popular area to float, and the section from Warren downstream can be crowded with inner-tubers in the summer but there is enough water to spread out and find very good fishing. Often to find secluded areas to fish, I'll head for the sides of these islands opposite of the area most canoes and tubers are floating. There is so much water in this part of the James that even the narrow sides of the islands carry enough water for great fishing. Take out on the left side of the river downstream from the Route 20 bridge just off Route 6.

The 5.8-mile float from Scottsville to Hardware Wildlife Management Area is very popular with anglers, canoeists and tubers. However, I've had some excellent fishing in this area. I prefer the downstream part of this float because it is loaded with islands showing a broad variety of water types allowing me to fish both topwater and underwater patterns. The take-out is on the left bank off Route 646 just above the mouth of the Hardware River.

I have many angling friends who drive great distances to float the 6.9-mile stretch from Hardware to New Canton. The numerous islands and strong riffles make this one of the most attractive and productive stretches of the James. Early in the season many anglers find that using fast sinking-tip fly lines with nymphs and streamers in these fast runs gives them many large smallmouths. Take out on the right below the Route 15 bridge.

The 11-mile float from New Canton to Columbia covers much flat water and the best smallmouth action will be found in the few riffles this stretch holds and along the shaded banks in the fastest runs. One day in late summer we started fishing one of these stretches with fast runs just as it was becoming daylight. The action was very good and we expected great fishing all day. But as the sun warmed the stream throughout the day the fishing became slower and slower.

Since the James River is so long giving the sun a chance to cook these lower reaches when they are already warm in August one will almost invariably get better smallmouth fishing early in the mornings. The take-out is at the Route 690 bridge on the right side.

The stretch from Columbia to Cartersville covers 9.5 miles with some very attractive scenery. Because of the flat nature of this water many anglers just float on through the slowest water and spend most of their time fishing the faster stretches. The take-out spot is on the right bank just downstream of the Route 45 bridge.

Launching at Carterville and floating to West View provides 5 miles of fairly slow water. The best action in this stretch is usually around the grass beds with surface bugs and shiner minnow imitations. Take out on the left bank just across from the island at Route 643.

From West View to Maidens you have a 12.5-mile float through great smallmouth water. The speed of the current increases with the gradient, and there are many great riffles where most of us prefer to beach the canoe and wade and fish with nymphs and streamers. Use caution when wading these strong runs; I had a friend get in trouble here when he was swept off his feet into a deep pool. Fortunately he was able to swim into an eddy before his waders filled. This is part of the reason I prefer to wade-wet in all of our smallmouth rivers the summer. Take out on the right above the Route 522 bridge.

Floating from Maidens to Watkins takes you through 13.1 miles of water with many different types of cover. The upper 10 miles has many fast riffles and numerous islands while the last 3 1/2 miles is flat water backed up by the Bosher Dam. I've had excellent fishing for nice-sized smallmouths by wading the upper areas and fishing the deep runs with streamers, and especially working the right bank with surface bugs. Take out on the right bank at Route 652.

The James River is an excellent stream and one needs only explore it to find the type fishing he likes.

FACILITIES

CANOE RENTAL:
James River Runners
10082 Hatton Ferry Rd.
Scottsville, VA 24590
Phone: (804) 286-2338

James River Reeling & Rafting
P.O. Box 757
265 Ferry St.
Scottsville, VA 24590
Phone: (804) 286-4386
(also camping)

CAMPGROUNDS:
Yogi Bear's Jellystone Park
Rt. 1 Box 61
1164 Middle Creek Rd.
Buchanan, VA 24066
Phone: (540) 254-2176

Wildwood Campground
6252 Elon Rd.
Monroe, VA 24574
Phone: (804) 299-5228

BED & BREAKFAST:
Chester
243 James River Rd.
Scottsville, VA 24590
Phone: (804) 286-3960

The Berkley House
64 Old Hollow Rd.
Buchanan, VA 24066
Phone: (540) 254-2548

MOTELS:
Lumpkins Motel
P.O. Box 68
1075 Valley St. Rt. 20
Scottsville, VA 24590
Phone: (804) 286-3690

Courtyard by Marriott
4640 Murray Place
Lynchburg, VA 24502
Phone: (804) 846-7900

Chapter 4
Roanoke (Staunton) River

The Staunton River is excellent for smallmouth bass fishing from Brookneal upstream and for largemouth fishing from there downstream, and is well known for the impoundments of the Leesville Dam and Kerr Reservoir. Much of this river flows through a remote part of Virginia where access areas other than those shown on the map must be gained by obtaining landowner permission.

Let's look at the access areas shown on the map and the type of fishing one can expect in these parts of the river.

The first popular float trip is the 11-mile stretch from Long Island to Brookneal since the access below the Leesville Dam is for bank fishing only. The river level will fluctuate with the water release from the dam so be observant. The put-in spot at Long Island is on the north side of the river at Route 761. In addition to the fine smallmouth and Roanoke bass fishing in this area, there are seasonal runs of striped bass, walleye and white bass.

The great fishing is complemented by some of the most beautiful country in Virginia for this stretch is designated as the scenic river portion by the State.

There is good smallmouth fishing in the riffles above and below the launch area so work these carefully before floating on downstream. There are several stretches of fast currents in this float that one needs to respect when floating the river. These do, however, provide great smallmouth fishing so consider beaching your canoe on the bank and fish them by wad-

The Roanoke (Staunton) River is a popular stream to float. It varies greatly from its upper to lower reaches.

ing. Take out on the left at Route 501 below the bridge.

The float from Brookneal to Watkins Bridge covers 28.6 miles except for a small take-out spot at Clarkston bridge on Route 620 which is 7 miles downstream from Brookneal. These long floats are popular with anglers who like to camp along the river. Since this is private land one should take time prior to the trip to obtain landowner permission to camp.

There are many islands in this stretch which add variety to the float and excellent largemouth fishing with surface bugs. Late in the summer when the aquatic grass beds are well

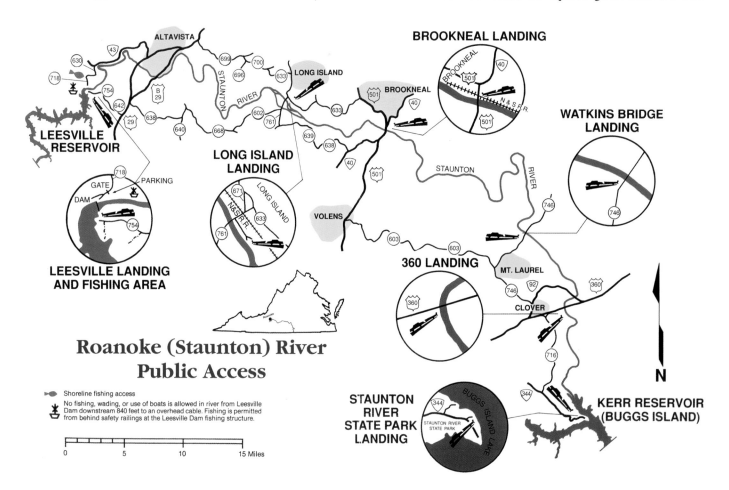

ALTAVISTA
LONG ISLAND
BROOKNEAL
BROOKNEAL LANDING
WATKINS BRIDGE LANDING
STAUNTON RIVER
LEESVILLE RESERVOIR
LONG ISLAND LANDING
VOLENS
LEESVILLE LANDING AND FISHING AREA
360 LANDING
MT. LAUREL
CLOVER
STAUNTON RIVER STATE PARK LANDING
KERR RESERVOIR (BUGGS ISLAND)

Roanoke (Staunton) River Public Access

🐟 Shoreline fishing access
No fishing, wading, or use of boats is allowed in river from Leesville Dam downstream 840 feet to an overhead cable. Fishing is permitted from behind safety railings at the Leesville Dam fishing structure.

0   5   10   15 Miles

N

formed one can often spot bass chasing minnows along the edges of the grass and in the open bays which form within them, especially early in the mornings and late in the evenings. These are often large fish so get a fly to them the second you spot this action. My favorites are the Shenandoah Sliders on the surface and the Silver Outcast Streamer underwater. Take out at the Route 746 bridge at Watkins.

The float from Watkins Bridge to the U.S. 360 bridge covers 8.9 miles and gives you a chance to take largemouth bass, Kentucky spotted bass, Roanoke bass, and during the seasonal runs, striped bass, white bass and walleye. Numerous small feeder streams enter the river in this stretch which can put extra food into the stream and promote extra feeding. Black Walnut Creek coming in on the right in the upper part of this stretch and Sandy Creek coming in from the left, several miles above the take-out, are excellent examples.

The numerous islands in this float deserve special attention. Since much of this float is almost directly south one has good shade around these islands in the mornings and evenings on opposite sides. Largemouths feed well on the surface in the shaded areas so fish them carefully. Take out at the ramp beside Route US 360 E on the right side.

From US 360 to the Staunton River State Park Ramp is 12.3 miles. Many anglers make an overnight trip out of this, but as mentioned before be sure to obtain landowner permission for camping. This is an exceptionally productive section for anglers who fish the banks with surface bugs as they float along. The most efficient tactic here is to take turns between paddling and fishing in order not to spook the bass with the extra splashing when you try to fish and paddle the canoe at the same time. In the slower lower part of this float you can pick up some large largemouths and crappie. The former will take surface bugs well, but I usually do best with small streamers for the crappie. The last 5 miles of this float are through flat water before reaching the take-out spot at the park on the right bank at the end of Route 344. If you like to observe wildlife you have a good chance to see bald eagles, osprey and numerous wading birds around the park.

The Roanoke (Staunton) River provides anglers with much of the action we find in our other large rivers, but the added attraction of the "bonus fish" running upstream from the Kerr Reservoir gives this fine stream a special appeal.

The smallmouths in the upper section of the Staunton River seem to prefer streamers and nymphs fished deeply.

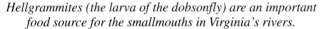

Hellgrammites (the larva of the dobsonfly) are an important food source for the smallmouths in Virginia's rivers.

Chapter 5
New River

The New River is one of the finest smallmouth streams in Virginia. It begins in the Blue Ridge Mountains in North Carolina, swings north into Virginia then meanders through a great variety of terrain for about 160 miles before leaving the Old Dominion to enter West Virginia and eventually flow into the Mississippi River.

It is the oldest river in North America. In fact, it is the second oldest river in the world with only the Nile River in Africa being older.

The New has a reputation for producing large fish as shown by the four state records it holds for a 45-pound muskellunge, a 7-pound 7-ounce smallmouth bass, a 2-pound 2-ounce yellow perch and a 14-pound 6-ounce walleye.

The volume of water which the New carries, its abundance of food and the ease of access lead Virginia's fisheries biologists to predict that the New will produce many more record fish. It holds good populations of smallmouth bass, largemouth bass, rock bass, white bass, spotted bass, striped bass, hybrid striped bass, walleye, muskellunge, yellow perch, black crappie, bluegill and redbreast sunfish.

The New River Trail State Park parallels the river from Pulaski to Fries or Galax providing excellent access for fishing, hiking and bicycling for over 50 miles.

There are five dams on the New River but many can be easily portaged. These dams are used to generate electricity so be ready to move to the side of the river if you notice a sudden rise of water level.

The access sites on the map of the New River that are designated with letters are informal sites which are suitable for canoes and small john boats. Please respect the private property around all launch sites by keeping them clean and not trespassing on private land.

In order to make the best showing on the New River one needs to be resourceful in adapting his fly patterns and tactics to the particular stretch he is fishing. Surface bugs, streamers and nymphs all produce well on the New. Due to the strong currents in certain parts of the river some anglers often resort to fast sinking-tip lines to aid in getting the streamers and nymphs to the bottom. Popular flies include: Silver Outcast Streamer, Black Strymph, Olive Strymph, Murray's Madtom, Clouser's Deep Sculpin, Whitlock's Sculpin, Spuddler, Bitch Creek Nymph, Casual Dress Nymph, Murray's Hellgrammite, Shenandoah Blue Popper, Chartreuse Slider, Murray's Yellow Darter, Tapply Hair Bug and Whitlock's Mouserat. All of these are effective on the New River in sizes 4, 6 and 8.

In order for you to get an overview of the New River so you can fish the areas which appeal most to you using the map on page 27, let's start at the upper reaches and float the whole

Often the best smallmouth fishing is found along the banks where the smallmouths find shade, food and cover.

river. We'll touch on the difference in the water and some of the tactics which are effective in different areas.

Starting at the Mouth of Wilson you can launch your canoe close to the intersection of Routes 93 and 58 on the west bank. You have about one mile of slow water upstream of Fields Dam which holds a good population of smallmouth bass and musky. Poppers work well on the shaded banks for the smallmouths and the musky can be tempted with large streamers on a sinking-tip fly line. Portage the dam on the left side. Fox Creek provides cool water where it enters just below the dam and can spark the smallmouth action during the summer. This total float is about 6 miles to the take-out point on the left bank just above the Route 601 bridge at Bridle Creek.

From Bridle Creek to Independence is 10 miles of prime smallmouth water. The numerous riffles and rapids here provide a great habitat for both minnows and hellgrammites, prompting many anglers to beach the canoe and work the water carefully with flies such as Shenk's White Streamer to match the minnows and Murray's Hellgrammite to mimic the natural hellgrammites. The take-out at Independence is on the left side just downstream of the Route 21 bridge.

From Independence to Baywood is 12 miles of fairly flat water which holds a good population of rock bass and spotted bass both of which will take small nymphs and streamers very well. Smallmouth action is best in this area below the riffles and on the banks where there is a strong current. As you approach the Route 58 bridge you can take-out on the right side of the river.

The 8.5-mile float from Baywood to Riverside takes you through slower water in the upper section, but several miles upstream from Riverside there is great smallmouth fishing around Joyce's Rapids. Consider beaching your canoe and fishing this area thoroughly with nymphs and streamers. During the latter part of the summer the smallmouth fishing can be very good where Elk Creek cools the river just above the take-out site. If you would like to float the river for two days and spend the night along the river there are good camping facilities close to Riverside. You can take your canoe out on the left side of the river close to the intersection of Routes 94 and 274.

From Riverside to Oldtown is a 6-mile float. Fish the shaded side of these islands with deer-hair surface bugs and poppers for smallmouths and panfish. There are numerous grass beds in this area which are loaded with minnows. Select those edges with the strongest currents brushing by the grass beds and fish them carefully with streamers such as the Silver Outcast and the Olive Strymph. Two miles downstream of the Route 94 bridge the take-out is on the right bank.

There is a good 2.5-mile float from Oldtown to Fries Dam (A) if you would like to catch some nice-sized largemouth bass and possibly a musky. When you see the blue barrels strung across the river prepare to take-out on the left bank because you are approaching the dam. There is a public wayside off Route 94 up the foot trail.

From Fries to the Byllesby Reservoir is a 7-mile float. Launch your canoe on the north side of the river in the town of Fries at Riverside Park. Many anglers find great smallmouth

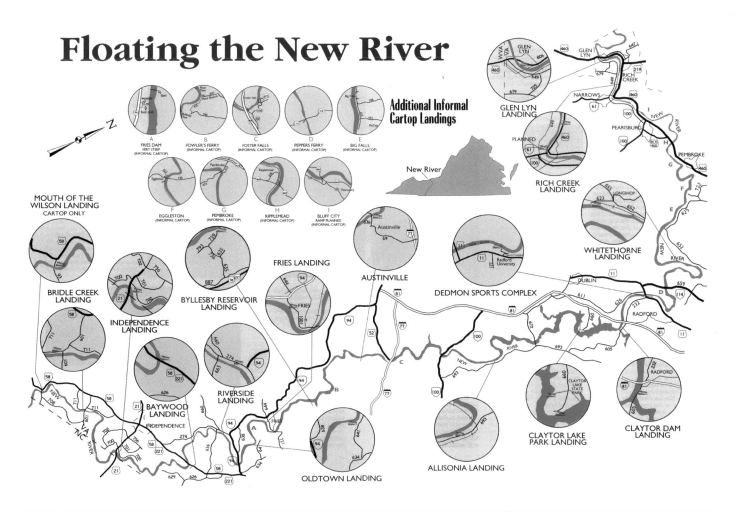

Floating the New River

action by fishing the water in the 1/2-mile stretch up under the Fries Dam before heading downstream. There is also very good fishing for musky from Fries Dam to the low-water bridge. There is excellent smallmouth water all the way downstream to the deep water behind Byllesby Dam. An especially good area is Double Shoals which lies about one mile below the low water bridge at Fries. Fishing poppers and streamers in the shallow sections here in early June and July and September and October can give you some memorable action. Be sure to pay special attention to that part of the river below Double Shoals where Bush Creek enters from the left and Chestnut Creek and Crooked Creek enter from the right. In addition to cooling the river during the summer these feeders can often add extra food for the bass and spark their feeding. You can take-out at the ramp at the end of Route 739 near Riverhill which is one mile upstream of the Byllesby Dam.

Launching at Fowler's Ferry (B) at Route 635 you have a 7.5-mile float through a very productive and attractive section of the New River. The last two state-record walleye, which were both over 14 pounds, came from this area. There is excellent smallmouth surface bug fishing around the numerous islands, and the riffles produce well with nymphs and streamers. Musky can also be taken in the deep pools here. There is a good take-out ramp at the Route 636 bridge at Austinville.

I strongly recommend the float from Austinville to Fosters Falls, it is only 3.5 miles but the smallmouth action is great, especially below Fosters Falls. The New River Trail State Park is adjacent to the river here. Foster Falls Village and the well-preserved shot tower at Jackson Ferry one mile upstream are all well worth visiting. You can take-out either above or below Foster Falls.

The 13.5-mile float from Fosters Falls (C) to Allisonia gives you the chance to catch large spotted bass, walleye and smallmouth bass in some of the finest water in the state. Allow extra time to carefully fish the heavy riffles with nymphs and streamers. Fish the grass beds between the Route 100 Bridge and Allisonia very carefully with streamers and poppers. There is also some excellent fishing for striped bass that run this area from late April to early June. The take-out site is off Route 693 at Allisonia.

Claytor Lake lies downstream from Allisonia. The Claytor Lake State Park is 472 acres and holds four campgrounds, cottages, hiking trails and a marina. This is an excellent area for a family vacation or for camping while fishing this section of the New River.

One should be aware on the float trips and when wading downstream from the Clayton Dam that this is used for generating electricity and there can be a sudden two to three foot rise

Healthy smallmouths like this are found throughout the whole New River drainage and they hit a fly with gusto.

in the water level. If you are wading mid-stream and notice an increase in the river level head to the side of the river.

By launching below Claytor Dam off Route 605 on the east side of the river and floating down to the Dedmon Sports Complex of Radford University you cover about 6 miles of my favorite water. Before heading downstream paddle up to Claytor Dam and carefully fish the rocky banks with nymphs and streamers. There is excellent smallmouth and spotted bass fishing up under the dam. I've had great smallmouth fishing right in the city of Radford by fishing streamers and poppers tight to the banks and around the islands. This is big water so consider going to a fast sinking-tip fly line to help you get your streamers and nymphs down in the heaviest runs.

By launching at the Dedmon Sports Complex of Radford University and floating to Peppers Ferry (D) you have about 5 miles of good smallmouth fishing. Muskellunge are stocked from Claytor Dam to the West Virginia line so be on the look-out for them. If you would like to get serious about taking a large musky on a fly rod go to a 9-weight rod with a sinking-tip line and 2/0 long, slim streamers. The ostrich herl streamers which are 5 to 7 inches long which Ron Kommer and I developed many years ago are excellent as are the Brooks' Blondes. Musky have sharp teeth so add a 6-inch shock tippet of 50-pound-test mono or wire to prevent getting nipped off. Take out on the left side of the river above the Route 114 bridge at Peppers Ferry (D).

From Peppers Ferry (D) to Whitethorne is an 8.5-mile float with some great smallmouth fishing below the fast water at Arsenal Rapids. At Whitethorne you can take-out on the right side of the river off Route 623.

The Whitethorne to Big Falls (E) float covers 7 miles of water considered by many to be the best smallmouth bass water in the state. A biologist friend who knows this river well says that smallmouth in the 2- to 4-pound class are common in this stretch. Large musky are also often landed in this stretch. At the lower end of this float you'll come to a great smallmouth rapid called Big Falls. Give this plenty of time and expect good action. You can take-out along Route 625 either above or below Big Falls.

The float from Big Falls (E) to Eggleston (F) is only 2.5 miles but serious anglers can easily devote a full day to fishing here by wading the best-looking runs, riffles and banks. One very productive area is the heavy water below the island on the right side of the river about one mile above the bridge at Eggleston. For this float you can put in along Route 625 on the right bank either above or below the falls and take-out on the left bank just upstream of the Eggleston bridge (Route 730) along Route 622.

From Eggleston (F) to Pembroke (G) is 6 miles of some of the finest smallmouth fly-fishing water you can find. The water is easy to wade, and a beginning angler can take many fish by casting a streamer, such as a Black Strymph or a Spuddler, down and across stream and swimming it through the riffles. You can put in along Route 622 above the Eggleston bridge on the left side and take-out off Route 623 on the right side of the river upstream of the bridge.

The float from Pembroke (G) to Ripplemead (H) is only 2 miles which provides time for wading and fishing the area thoroughly. Put in off Route 623 on the right side of the river above the bridge and take-out on the left bank off Route 636 just under the Route 460 bridge.

From Ripplemead (H) to Bluff City (I) is a beautiful 7.5-mile float. Put in under the Route 460 bridge off Route 636. About one mile below the bridge begins a series of strong riffles which provide great smallmouth action. I like to beach the canoe above the riffles to wade and fish them with streamers and nymphs. Another set of excellent riffles are about one mile below where Big Stony Creek comes in on the right. Clendennin Shoals is the fastest rapids in this area holding many large smallmouth so save time to fish it thoroughly. Take-out close to Bluff City on the left side below the Route 460 bridge.

The Bluff City to Rich Creek float is 5.5 miles. There is a fair amount of flat water in this float, but be careful at Narrows Falls below the town of Narrows. There is a rapid drop of about 7 feet here followed quickly by the remains of an old crumbled dam that can be dangerous. There is excellent fishing for smallmouths and rock bass where Wolf Creek comes in at Narrows. Take-out just below Narrows Falls on the right bank.

The Rich Creek to Glen Lyn is a beautiful 5-mile float. Put in on the right bank off Route 460 downstream of Narrows Falls. The large islands and gentle riffles in this area provide a broad variety of cover which enable us to have good smallmouth and rock bass fishing with nymphs, streamers and surface bugs. This is the last float on the New River in Virginia with public take-out sites. The Glen Lyn take-out is just above the Route 460 Bridge on the right side at a very nice small park.

Many of the launch sites listed here provide excellent fishing by wading. Since the New is such a large river it is easy to wade in at one of these sites and fish all day without ever casting to the same spot twice, then return to your car that evening. Remember, however, the land around these sites is private so treat it with respect, entering and leaving at the designated area.

FACILITIES

CANOE RENTAL:

New River Adventures
1007 North 4th St.
Wytheville, VA 24382
Phone: (540) 228-8311 or
(540) 699-1034

New River Canoe & Campground Inc.
3770 New River Parkway
Independence, VA 24348
Phone: (540) 773-3412

CAMPGROUNDS:

Claytor Lake State Park
4400 State Park Rd.
Dublin, VA 24084
Phone: (540) 674-5492 or
1-800-933-7275

New River Trail State Park
RR 2 Box 126F
Foster Falls, VA 24360
Phone: (540) 699-6778

BED & BREAKFAST:

Boxwood Inn
460 E. Main St.
Wytheville, VA 24382
Phone: (540) 228-8911

The Oaks (Victorian Inn)
311 E. Main St.
Christiansburg, VA 24073
Phone: (540) 381-1500

MOTELS/HOTELS:

Evergreen Lodge
139 Evergreen Lane
Independence, VA 24348
Phone: (540) 773-2859

Ramada Motel
955 Pepper's Ferry Rd
Wytheville VA 24382
Phone: (540) 228-6000

Chapter 6
Clinch River

There are several characteristics of the Clinch River which make it one of my favorite smallmouth streams that may also be important to you as you consider locations for your next outing. There is excellent access over its 135 miles which enable you to fish different areas on almost every trip. Lying in the remote southwest corner of the Old Dominion the Clinch is not close to any large population centers so you frequently have long stretches of river to yourself. But possibly the greatest appeal the Clinch River has for me personally is the willingness of some of the largest smallmouths to strike surface bugs. One of the largest smallmouths I've ever seen took my Shenandoah Blue Popper just above Nash's Ford late one July evening.

This area is very rich in history. Daniel Boone lived for some time near the village of Castlewood and used the Clinch River in many ways.

Biologically the Clinch has several unique characteristics.

It contains over 100 species of fish, which is more than any other river in Virginia, as well as having about 50 species of mussels which is more than any other river in the world. Also, this river and its tributaries are the only waters in Virginia that hold saugers.

The popular game fish in the Clinch are the smallmouth bass, largemouth bass, rock bass, bluegill, redbreast sunfish, longear sunfish, black crappie, musky, with striped bass and white bass in the lower reaches.

Popular streamers for the Clinch River include the Spuddler, Silver Outcast, Murray's Madtom, Shenk's White Streamer, Clouser's Sculpin, Black Strymph, Olive Strymph and Olive Woolly Buggers. Productive nymphs include the Bitch Creek, Casual Dress, Murray's Hellgrammite and Damselfly. Effective surface bugs include the Shenandoah Blue Popper, Green Potomac Popper, Damsel Popper, Yellow Darter, Chartreuse Shenandoah Slider, Tapply Green/White Hair Bug and Whitlock's Near Nuff Frog.

In order for you to see just where the different types of water are on the Clinch let's set up an imaginary float trip that covers the river from its upper reaches to the Tennessee state

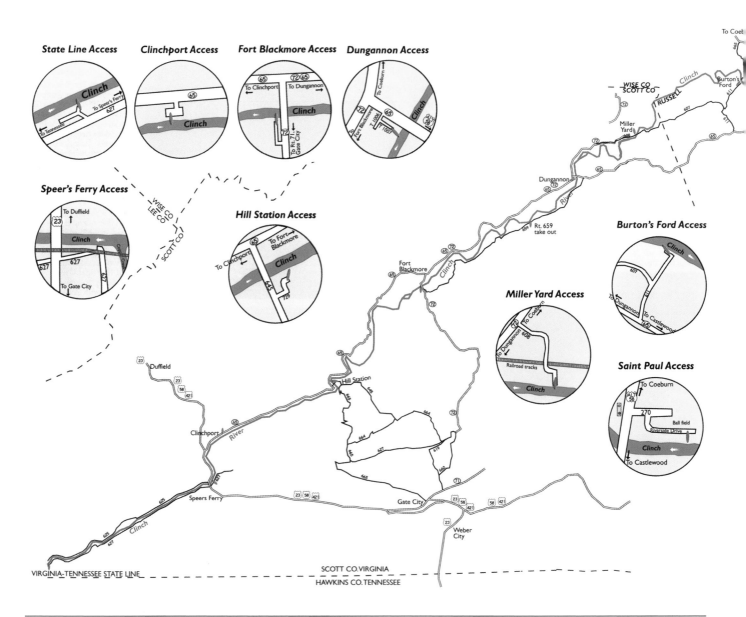

Clinch River Float Trips

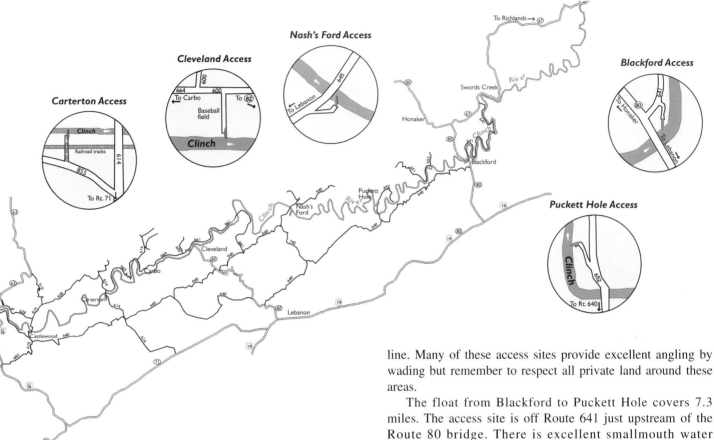

Carterton Access

Cleveland Access

Nash's Ford Access

Blackford Access

Puckett Hole Access

The Clinch River is one of the most beautiful rivers in Virginia and flows through one of the most beautiful parts of the country. It offers easy access and great fishing.

line. Many of these access sites provide excellent angling by wading but remember to respect all private land around these areas.

The float from Blackford to Puckett Hole covers 7.3 miles. The access site is off Route 641 just upstream of the Route 80 bridge. There is excellent smallmouth water throughout this area. Early in the season, nymphs and streamers are very productive below the riffles and in the deep runs. Sinking-tip lines are often a great help in working these flies across the bottom in the fast runs. You can take-out at the Puckett Hole landing which is off Route 652 on the right side of the river.

Floating from Puckett Hole to Nash's Ford takes you through 9 miles of some of the prettiest country and finest smallmouth water in Virginia. Put-in at Route 652 and take-out at Route 645 just above the bridge on the left side of the river. The first area of fast water on this float is just downstream of the confluence with Cedar Creek. This is excellent water to fish with streamers for smallmouths especially in May and June. A second section of very fast water is just upstream of the take-out point. I've had excellent smallmouth fishing here late in the summer when the river drops by fishing the grass beds and banks with the Shenandoah Blue Popper. There are some very large smallmouths in this area. If you happen to hit the previous two areas when there is a lot of water in the river you may want to portage them and fish below them.

The float from Nash's Ford to Cleveland covers 7.1 miles and has much less gradient than the float above Nash's Ford. Musky, walleye and sunfish are found in good numbers in this area. There are several sharp bends in the river in this section which can produce good smallmouth action to poppers fished tight against the shaded banks over cobblestone bottoms where the current is fast. Take out adjacent to the baseball field at Cleveland off Route 600 on the right side of the river.

From Cleveland to Carterton is 7.5 miles. There are several excellent deep pools in this float that hold good numbers of musky and walleye. Consider using a fast sinking-tip line to work these depths effectively. Long slim streamers and bucktails are very effective for musky. Remember to use a shock tippet of wire or 50-pound-test mono so the musky will not bite you off. The take-out site at Carterton is on the left bank off Route 855 just downstream of the Route 614 bridge.

The float from Carterton to Saint Paul covers 8 miles. The best areas for smallmouths here are in the riffles and runs where streamers and nymphs are a good bet. The aquatic grass

The smallmouths in the Clinch River show a decided preference for the fast water around riffles and ledges and if there are dense aquatic grass beds they like this even better.

beds which develop late in the summer to the sides and at the lower ends of these riffles can produce some excellent surface-bug fishing about dusk. There is good fishing for walleye and sunfish in the slower, deeper parts of this float. Take out on the right side of the river at Riverside Drive off Route 270 at Saint Paul.

There is some excellent smallmouth fishing in the 6.2-mile float between Saint Paul and Burton's Ford. Be sure to try hair bugs and poppers around the grass beds in the shallow areas around Saint Paul. This fishes best early in the morning and late in the evening. Just downstream of the railroad in Saint Paul there are some great fast-water riffles where nymphs and streamers produce great smallmouth action. There is another section of fast water downstream several miles that gives great smallmouth fishing. During the spring there is very good walleye fishing in this section. Take out at the Burton's Ford access site on the left which is just off Route 611.

The float from Burton's Ford to Miller's Yard is 7.1 miles of beautiful fast-flowing river through an attractive remote area. There are numerous good riffles and several falls throughout this area assuring good smallmouth and walleye fishing. Allow time to beach your canoe to wade and fish the runs and riffles carefully. Take out on the right side of the river at Route 608 below the railroad.

Floating from Miller's Yard to Dungannon covers 3.7 miles of high-gradient water containing many large smallmouths. Walleye and sunfish are also abundant in this stretch and if you would like to catch a sauger this is one of the best areas. Take out just downstream of the Route 65 bridge on the right at Dungannon.

You can launch your canoe at Dungannon and float downstream for 3 to 5 miles depending on where you take-out along Route 659. Route 659 parallels the river for several miles so there are numerous areas to take-out depending on your schedule. Be sure to get landowner permission for using these take-out spots. There is some good fast smallmouth water in the upper part of this area which fishes well with streamers early in the season. From the middle to the latter part of the season the grass beds and shaded banks produce well with poppers and deer hair bugs. The deep pools in this float offer you a good chance to take musky, sauger and walleye.

By putting in along Route 659 and floating to Fort Blackmore you will cover about 8 to 10 miles depending on where you launch. This is a low-gradient part of the river so it fishes better for walleye and musky than it does for smallmouths. In fact there is a five-mile-long pool here that averages 14 feet deep called 'the retck'. If you are serious about musky this is your pool. Fish it deeply and slowly with a fast sinking-tip line using long streamers. Added attractions in this area are the striped bass and white bass that work their way upstream from the Norris Reservoir in Tennessee. You can take your canoe out just downstream of the Route 72 bridge on the left side of the river at Fort Blackmore.

From Fort Blackmore to Hill Station is a 7.9-mile float through some of the most beautiful country in Virginia. There is good smallmouth fishing with surface bugs around

A wonderful trait of the large bass in the Clinch River is their willingness to hit surface bugs. Fish them slowly against the shaded banks and along the edges of the grass beds.

Pendelton Island in the upper part of this section. The deep, slow pools a little further downstream hold good populations of musky, walleye and sauger. Your take-out point is just upstream of the Route 645 bridge off Route 729 on the left side of the river at Hill Station.

The float from Hill Station to Clinchport is 5.2 miles of fairly slow water populated mostly with sunfish. The faster riffles and some of the stronger runs along the cobblestone banks offer the best smallmouth fishing. You can take your canoe out at Clinchport along Route 65 on the right side of the river.

The Clinchport to Speer's Ferry is a good section to float with many great areas to wade. It covers just 2 miles so it is ideal for a fly-angler to work the riffles and runs for small-mouths. The deep cuts between the ledges provide you a good chance to take sauger and walleye on streamers. Take out at Speer's Ferry on the left side of the river off Route 627 close to the railroad bridge.

The float from Speer's Ferry to State Line is 9 miles of beautiful water to finish our trip to the Tennessee line. Be sure to take your camera because the scenery is outstanding. Most of the smallmouths in this section are just above and below the riffles and in the grass beds where the current is fast.

If you spend some time exploring the Clinch River I believe you may easily develop the respect for it that I have.

FACILITIES

CAMPGROUNDS:
Flag Rock Recreation Area
City of Norton
  Rt. 619
  Norton, VA 24273
  Phone: (540) 679-0754

Natural Tunnel State Park
  Rt. 3 Box 250
  Duffield, VA 24224
  Phone: (540) 940-2674

Clinch Ranger District
9416 Darden Drive
Wise, VA 24293
Phone: (540) 328-2931
Three Campgrounds: Cave Springs,
  High Knob and Bark Camp

BED & BREAKFAST:
Summerfield Inn
  101 West Valley St.
  Abingdon, VA 24210
  Phone: (540) 628-5905 or
  1-800-668-5905

Inn on Town Creek
  445 E Valley St.
  Abingdon, VA 24210
Phone: (540) 628-4560

Our House Inn
Lick Creek Rd.
Rt. 1, Box 593
Clincho, VA 24226
Phone: (540) 835-9634 or (540)
865-5150

MOTELS:
Ramada Inn
  P.O. Box 260
  US 58 & 421 West
  Duffield, VA 24244
  Phone: (540) 431-4300

Holiday Inn
551 Highway 58 E
Norton, VA 24273
Phone: (540) 679-7000 or 1-800-
465-4329

CABINS:
Abram's Branch Cabin & Forest
  Res.
  P.O. Box 1210
  St. Paul, VA 24283

Chapter 7
Shenandoah National Park

Fishing in the Shenandoah National Park is special to those of us who fish it regularly. Special because it contains many beautiful mountain streams that provide some of the finest stream fishing for wild brook trout on the East Coast. Special because of the colorful history of the area. But, possibly, the most special aspects about fishing the Shenandoah National Park are those which President Herbert Hoover referred to when he had his fishing camp here while he was the President of the United States. He writes, "Fishing is a chance to wash one's soul with pure air, with the rush of the brook, or with the shimmer of the sun on the blue water."

For me, fishing in the Shenandoah National Park is more than catching beautiful wild trout, more than inhaling its striking beauty, more than sinking into its peaceful solitude; it is a filling, of a previously undetected void, with an emotion of complete satisfaction that only God can give.

Shenandoah National Park History

The Shenandoah National Park was officially formed on December 26, 1935 when Secretary of the Interior Harold Ickes accepted the deed from the Commonwealth of Virginia conveying 176,429 acres to the Federal Government.

Things were rolling well prior to this for in 1933 and 1934 about 1,000 young men of the newly formed Civilian Conservation Camp (CCC) were stationed here in six separate camps. Their primary tasks were to build trails and shelters, to fight fires, work to reduce fire hazards, control erosion and work on the Skyline Drive.

The Skyline Drive is a meandering road that travels the crest of the Park's mountains for about one hundred miles providing many pull-offs where one can park and look west into the beautiful Shenandoah Valley or east into the sprawling Piedmont area of Virginia which feathers off to the Atlantic Ocean.

The opening of the Skyline Drive on September 15, 1934 was especially important to anglers for it made available the headwaters of the fine brook trout streams. Today, some of the best fishing is gained by parking at the locations I'll give you as we cover each stream and hiking from one to four miles down the mountains into the streams and then fishing back up the mountain. Even though the Shenandoah National Park is only a two-hour drive from our nation's capital one can still hike into these hollows and fish all day without seeing another angler.

Seasons

Good trout fishing usually begins in the park in mid-March when the water temperature stays above forty degrees for several days. Some years the streams may be quite full at this

The beautiful mountains of the Shenandoah National Park beckon anglers to try the numerous wild-trout streams.

When viewing the striking beauty of the inspiring dogwood trees which drape the mountains of the Shenandoah National Park, one can easily understand the pride with which Virginian's claim this as their state flower.

Major Mayfly Hatches in Virginia's Mountain Streams

INSECT	MAR.	APR.	MAY	JUNE	JULY	ANGLERS NAME	ARTIFICIAL DRY	ARTIFICIAL NYMPH
Epeorus pleuralis	●					Quill Gordon	Quill Gordon 12, 14 Mr. Rapidan 12, 14	Quill Gordon 12, 14 Mr. Rapidan 12, 14
Paralepto-phlebia adaptiva		●				Dark Blue Quill	Blue Quill 16, 18	Blue Quill 16
Stenonema vicarium		●				March Brown	March Brown 12, 14 Mr. Rapidan 12, 14	March Brown 12, 14
Stenonema fuscum			●			Gray Fox	Gray Fox 14 Ginger Quill 14	Gray Fox 14 March Brown 14
Stenonema canadense			●			Light Cahill	Light Cahill Gray Yellow N. H. 16	Light Cahill 14
Ephemerella dorothea				●		Sulphur	Fox Sulphur 16, 18 Gray Yellow N.H. 16, 18	Sulphur 16, 18 Pheasant Tail 16, 18

Major Caddisfly and Stonefly Hatches in Virginia's Mountain Streams

INSECT	APR.	MAY	JUNE	JULY	AUG.	SEPT.	ANGLERS NAME	ARTIFICIAL DRY	ARTIFICIAL NYMPH
Brachy-centrus (Caddisfly)	●						American Grannom	Elk Hair Caddis, Olive 14, 16	Olive Pupa 14
Rhyacophila (Caddisfly)			●				Green Sedge	Elk Hair Caddis, Olive 14, 16	Green Larva 14
Pycnopsyche Caddis (Caddisfly)						●	Brown Sedge Stick Bait (local)	Elk Hair Caddis, Brown 14, 16	Brown Pupa 12, 14
Isoperla bilineata (Stonefly)		●					Yellow Sally Little Yellow Stonefly	Little Yellow Stonefly 16, 18 Light Goofus 16	Red Squirrel Nymph 16 Little Yellow Stonefly 16
Pteronarcys dorsata (Stonefly)	●						Giant Black Stonefly	Improved Sofa Pillow 6	Brooks Dark Stonefly Nymph 8, 10

Terrestrial Insects in Virginia's Trout Streams

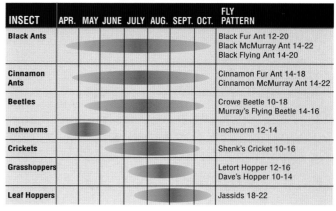

INSECT	APR.	MAY	JUNE	JULY	AUG.	SEPT.	OCT.	FLY PATTERN
Black Ants		●	●	●	●			Black Fur Ant 12-20 Black McMurray Ant 14-22 Black Flying Ant 14-20
Cinnamon Ants		●	●	●	●	●		Cinnamon Fur Ant 14-18 Cinnamon McMurray Ant 14-22
Beetles		●	●	●	●	●		Crowe Beetle 10-18 Murray's Flying Beetle 14-16
Inchworms	●	●						Inchworm 12-14
Crickets			●	●	●			Shenk's Cricket 10-16
Grasshoppers				●	●	●		Letort Hopper 12-16 Dave's Hopper 10-14
Leaf Hoppers				●	●	●		Jassids 18-22

time, and we get our best fishing by parking on the Skyline Drive and hiking down the mountains to the upper reaches of the streams. If you don't like the steep climb back up the mountain after fishing all day, an option is to park at the lower reaches of the streams and hike several miles up the mountain in order to get above some of the feeder streams before you start fishing. Then at the end of the day you hike downhill.

The best aquatic insect hatches occur in the Park in April and May and by following the accompanying hatch charts and the recommended matching flies, the fishing can be outstanding. If you are like some anglers and want to simplify your fly selection the Mr. Rapidan Dry Fly in sizes 14 and 16 is an excellent fly to use in March, April and May. I developed this pattern about twenty years ago to match the general body coloration of the Quill Gordon and March Brown mayflies while providing excellent angler visibility, and I must admit it seldom lets us down.

By June the Park streams are low and clear requiring a more cautious approach to prevent scaring the trout. But once one adapts his tactics, tackle and fly patterns to meet the whims of the trout, the entire summer can provide outstanding action. If fact, many experienced anglers prefer the summer season, feeling there is great gratification in mastering the challenges.

Fall trout fishing in the Park is usually excellent. The water temperatures are much more comfortable for the trout and they feed aggressively. The water levels are usually better and the brook trout apparently sense the demands spawning will soon place upon them. Basically, fall is one season you don't want to miss in the Park.

Food in Virginia's Mountain Trout Streams

A basic understanding of the natural foods available to trout in the mountain streams can often be beneficial when the trout become selective. The three following charts show you the foods which are more prevalent at each time period and the fly patterns which match them.

Tackle for Virginia's Mountain Trout Streams

Some of the finest trout fishing in Virginia is found in the small mountain streams.

Here, one should select rods which give accurate and delicate presentations in the fifteen- to thirty-foot range. Since there are often tree limbs close overhead short rods are preferred by most anglers. Thus, rods from 6 1/2 to 7 1/2 feet long that balance with two-, three- or four-weight lines are a good bet.

Fly reels should be lightweight but sturdy. A fall in these small streams usually sends the rod and reel crashing into the rocks and fragile reels have short life expectancies.

The selection of the proper leader for this close-in fishing is very important for often we are casting only the leader and a few feet of fly line. My personal favorite is a compound, knotted leader nine feet long tapering down to 4X, 5X and 6X depending on the fly size.

Floating lines will meet all of one's needs in these mountain streams. If you anticipate the need for many long casts you might want to consider a weight-forward taper. If you do a lot of roll casting you may prefer a double-taper line.

Hip-length boots are best for these small streams. I prefer the bootfoot style, but the stocking foot styles with separate wading shoes are fine. Just be sure you have a high-quality felt sole whichever style you choose. Chest-high waders are more than one needs and they are more uncomfortable than hippers if you plan to hike-in several miles.

I'll never again be without a high quality raincoat in the back of my vest as I head into these remote headwater streams. I found out the hard way just how uncomfortable—and potentially dangerous—it is to get soaked by a heavy rain three miles up in the mountains from the car.

Sculptured ice flows welcome anglers into the mountain headwater streams in the spring.

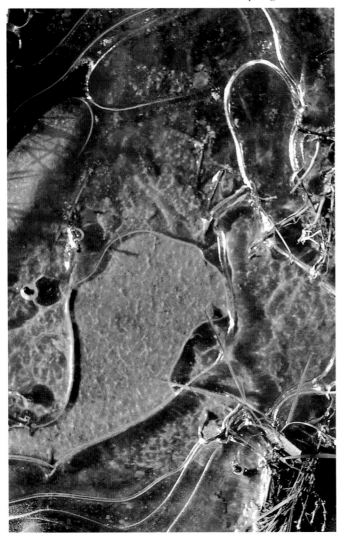

Backpacking in the Shenandoah National Park

It is not necessary to pack into the backcountry and spend a night or two in order to have good trout fishing in the Park. However, backpacking and mountain trout fishing blend well together, producing a very rewarding experience.

Not being rushed to head out of the hollows before darkness falls will enable you to take advantage of the abundance of aquatic insects present at dusk.

For example, my son Jeff and I recently packed into a Park stream I had fished often over the years and felt I knew well. The stretch we were on was a long hike from the closest road, and prior to our camping trip I have never been able to fish it until dusk. I respect rattlesnakes too much to hike very far in these mountains in the dark.

Having only about an hour to fish after setting up the tent we decided to fish until we could no longer see our flies on the water. There was a sparse mayfly dance over the stream, and a few spent Sulphur spinners were falling onto the surface. The first several pools all produced brookies which were located by seeing rise-forms. The later we fished the more flies fell onto the stream; more flies meant more rising fish, and soon there were feeding trout everywhere. The last pool I fished that evening was narrow and very long; the trout were in a line from the tail of the pool to the head, as if in a pre-determined tactical position to assure no spent Sulphur drifted all the way through the pool.

The fishing was outstanding because of the concentration of spent flies, and had we not been spending the night there, we would have missed it.

Backcountry camping will get you away from other anglers simply because of the amount of time required to reach a specific area. It also enables you to make the best use of your time.

Certain sections of some streams are so far from the closest access roads that to hike in, fish them and then hike out the same day would mean spending more time hiking than fishing.

Getting back away from the roads can also provide better fishing. Many serious Park anglers do not kill any of their fish, feeling that each trout is too valuable to be caught only once. However, some fellows still keep their trout; often the further you go into the backcountry, the more fish you find. There is one problem that can occur in this respect. Some backpackers talk romantically about how great it is to cook their freshly caught trout for the evening meal, proudly volunteering that they only kill what they plan to eat. The problem with this logic is that they fail to realize the negative impact this can have on these fragile streams if all backpacking anglers do the same thing.

No special fishing tackle is required when backpacking. However, since you will be carrying less than you usually do to lighten the load, each item should be carefully selected. Take only those items which have proven to be worthy for mountain trout fishing. This is no place to test that new rod, experiment with an unusual leader design or test a whole boxful of untried fly patterns. You don't have to take a lot of tackle but it had better be right or you will have a very frustrating trip.

Small, multi-piece pack rods are nice for this type fishing, but they are not a must. You should, however, make sure the rod you use in the little streams will load properly with a

The rich history of the Shenandoah National Park is just one of the subtle bonuses of fishing here.

number four or smaller line size. Have several extra leaders and ample tippet material. One medium-size fly box will hold all the flies you need. These should be selected to cover the specific needs you expect to encounter at the time of your trip.

Foot gear for this type hiking and fishing is a matter of personal preference. The main thing to keep in mind is that you want to have safe footing on the trails as well as in the streams. Injuries from bad falls are much more dangerous when they occur a long way from civilization. Be sure to carry a first-aid kit and a snakebite kit. A small whistle, capable of shrill blasts, is good insurance if you are alone.

Always let someone know where you will be; even if it's your family or fishing buddy back at home. If you do not show up at the appointed time at least someone will know where to look for you.

Getting lost in the Park's backcountry is a real possibility. I have gotten lost twice, and I can assure you it is a very uncomfortable feeling.

I once came across two fellows who were close to panic as they raced up a trail begging me to tell them where they were and how to get out. These fellows were miles from where they thought they were, and the shortest route I could plot for them to get back to the Skyline Drive still caused them to be five hours late in meeting their group. This whole problem resulted from a poorly sketched map.

Anyone camping, or even just fishing, the Park's backcountry should have a good set of maps. There are three maps which completely cover the park. These are designated as Northern, Central, and Southern Section Maps. They portray in detail, streams, elevations, trails, shelters, roads and facilities.

MAPS ARE AVAILABLE FROM:

Murray's Fly Shop
P.O. Box 156
Edinburg, VA 22824
(540) 984-4212
(540) 999-3582

Shenandoah Natural History Association
Shenandoah National Park
3655 US Hwy. 211 E
Luray, VA 22835

The following are some of the suggestions, rules and regulations governing backcountry camping as set forth by the Shenandoah National Park.

Think Ahead

When you explore the backcountry you have to live out of your knapsack. And you face what seems a contradiction: you must take everything you need for the trip yet travel light. Result: You get down to life's basic necessities in a hurry.

With such choices to make, you'll find it is important to plan your wilderness journey ahead of time. Here are some things to consider:

Compass: A good azimuth compass teams up well with a topographic map to give you the land navigation tools you need.

Backpack: Join in the lively discussions all backpackers enjoy about what makes the lightest, best balanced, most easily carried packboard, knapsack and frame, or rucksack— then make your own choice.

Clothing: Choose clothing that suits Shenandoah's changeable, cool, sometimes wet weather. Bring layers of clothes that can be peeled off. A rain poncho also makes a good ground cloth.

Sleeping bag: Select a warm one for cold nights yet lightweight for carrying.

Tent: Synthetic fabrics have made possible a variety of lightweight trail tents, although some hikers get along well with a tarpaulin as a simple shelter. A hammock can serve instead of a tent.

Food: Freeze-dried and dehydrated foods are light to carry and have revolutionized menus in the backcountry. No more hardtack and raisins; now you can turn out miracle meals fit for a king of the trail. From April to October, camping supplies are available at various locations in the park.

Tools of the trade: Items like a backpacker stove, matches, rope, camp knife, flashlight, canteen and collapsible water container quickly come to mind. Your list will expand to include other necessities, then shrink to exclude luxuries.

First Aid: You will want to take along a standard kit for possible on-the-trail treatment.

Emergency equipment: Depending on how deep into the wilderness you plan to go, you may carry along a mirror,

whistle or other emergency signaling items. In the winter, take additional clothing and rations.

Before you depart, it is a good idea to leave a copy of your planned itinerary, routes and time of return with your family or a close friend.

When You Reach the Park

Pick up your free backcountry permit (during daylight hours only) at an entrance station, at a ranger station, at one of the two park visitor centers or at park headquarters. Park headquarters is four miles west of Thornton Gap on U.S. Highway 211.

Permit

If you wish, you may get your backcountry permit ahead of time. Drop a brief letter to the Superintendent, Shenandoah National Park, Rt. 4 Box 293, Luray, VA 22835 (Attn: Backcountry Permit). Tell him the dates you will be in the Park, the number in your party, the location and dates of each overnight camp, and of course your name and address.

Issuing backcountry permits allows the Park staff to monitor and regulate the number of users in wilderness areas. Permits are an important management tool in the Park's plan of dispersed backcountry use.

At several ranger stations, wilderness hikers may view a five-minute slide talk "Backpacking in Shenandoah: What You'll Need To Know." A ranger will be on duty to answer questions concerning trail conditions, weather forecasts and interesting spots and hazards along the route.

You might also pick up a Park minifolder that gives an overall map of the Park, as well as another pocket-sized folder titled "Bear: Friend or Foe?"

With your permit, you and your party (maximum of 10 persons) may camp at nearly any isolated location you choose.

Backcountry Rules

Now that you are fully equipped and well prepared, there are 190,000 acres open to camping in the Park. Here are the common sense rules governing camping in the backcountry of Shenandoah National Park that the rangers will enforce:

*Permits are required and must be obtained before entering the backcountry.

*Backcountry camping is literally "out of sight!" Pitch your camp at least 250 yards away from any paved road and half a mile from any developed Park area. Fade into the wilderness by camping out of sight of any other camping party, and at least 25 yards from any stream.

*Do not plan to bed down in one of the trail shelters. They are for emergency use only—for first aid or protection in a severe storm. You're prepared to camp in the open—do your thing.

*Wood or charcoal fires are not permitted in the Shenandoah backcountry. Improper wood gathering, fire-blackened rocks and sterilized soil produce long-lasting damage to the environment. Instead, bring along one of the efficient and compact backpacker stoves.

The mayfly hatches in the Park can be very heavy in the spring, exciting both the trout and the anglers.

*Do not trench your tent or level off your tent site. Erase all evidence of your campsite when you leave. Treat the natural surroundings as gently as you can.

*Two days is the maximum stay at a backcountry campsite. Move along—so the vegetation can restore itself.

*Bearproof your campsite. Hang your food at a distance from your campsite and at least 10 feet above the ground. Choose a limb that cannot support a bear's weight; rig your food above the ground between two trees.

*Lighten your pack by leaving glass containers at home—they are prohibited in the backcountry.

*Horses must be tied near the tailside on a short tether. Free grazing is not permitted. Carry pellet feed for your horse.

*Riders must keep their mounts off foot trails and away from campgrounds and developed areas. Horses may be ridden on designated yellow blazed trails only.

*Pets are best left at home; any pets within the Park must be on a short leash, not allowed to run freely.

Violation of backcountry regulations can bring a minimum fine of $25. If you have questions, ask a ranger before you start.

Backcountry Sanitation

*Carry out all used cans, aluminum foil and disposables. (Empty cans are easier to carry if you flatten them.) Burying such trash is not satisfactory because it does not decompose and eventually comes to the surface through animal or frost action.

*Place all other refuse in plastic bags and pack it out; don't litter the landscape.

*To ensure safe drinking water, boil the water for ten minutes.

*After washing dishes or bathing, discard the water and detergent at least 30 feet away from any stream or spring. In this way, the earth will strain the chemicals and prevent stream pollution.

*A small hole should be dug to deposit human waste and covered.

Backcountry Trail Tips

*Stay on blazed trails unless you're proficient with your topographical map and compass.

*Team up with one or more companions for safety and comradeship.

*Children: if you have them along, be sure they have identification on them at all times; tell them what to do if they get lost ("stay where you are"); and give them a whistle to signal for help.

*Sign up at trail registers. It's a good safety measure and your information may help park managers learn more about backcountry use.

*In a lightning storm, move downhill below a ridge or a peak. Avoid exposed solitary objects such as large rocks or trees. Find shelter in lower areas, in a dense stand of trees, or under overhanging rocks.

*Limit the weight of your pack to one-fifth your own weight—until you prove you can carry more.

These wild spawning brook trout are the crown jewels of the Shenandoah National Park for the angler.

*Never take short cuts across switchbacks in the trail. It can be hazardous for you, can damage the vegetation and will cause soil erosion.

Last Word

Shenandoah's wilderness areas have been set aside as an outdoor museum of natural history. Man, as the intruder, should neither harm nor disturb the natural environment. By preparing for your backcountry visit and by exercising "good mountain manners" you will reserve the wilderness for those who come down the trail after you.

Book

The book *Trout Fishing in the Shenandoah National Park* listing twenty-eight trout steams, their access points and angling tactics is available from: Shenandoah Publishing Co., P.O. Box 156, Edinburg, VA 22824. Phone: (540) 984-4212

Chapter 8
Hughes River

The Hughes River drainage is one of the best trout fisheries in the Park. It is composed of three separate streams and thus offers a broad variety of angling opportunities. I will take advantage of this potential to show you how you can utilize different areas within the same watershed to improve your fishing.

For example, one early spring day I took a friend to the Hughes River and started him in the lower Park boundary and had him fish upstream. In order to give him the best water I told him I'd walk on up the trail two miles to where Hannah Run came in and I'd fish that and he could continue fishing on up the main part of the Hughes River if he got that far.

Hannah Run carries only about one-third the volume of the Hughes so I didn't expect outstanding fishing, but that is exactly what I got. Every pool had rising trout and I took several in almost every pool on a Mr. Rapidan size 14 dry fly. Admittedly, I forgot about my friend until quite late in the day. He is a very capable trout fisherman and I just assumed he was getting the same type wonderful action I was getting. However, when I met him that evening on the main part of the Hughes I was shocked when he told me he had landed only a few small trout all day and that he dug these out on nymphs. He said he had no strikes on drys and had not seen any trout rising.

Finally, for the first time that day, I took a serious look at the water he had been fishing, and I realized it was much too high for good fishing. My attempt to put my friend into the best water in the main stream, while I played around with the smaller feeder higher up in the mountain, had actually produced the opposite results of what I had anticipated.

Although this was an embarrassing way to learn the

An effective tactic on this stream in the summer and fall is to spot the trout in the pools and then go one on one with them.

importance of fishing the proper water level under various conditions I have never forgotten it and have taken advantage of it hundreds of times since then to help my students, other anglers and myself.

You see, almost every mountain freestone stream pulls its flow from numerous hollows, brooks and feeder streams so if you have too much water down low you simply head upstream or, if possible, approach the stream from a road leading into the upper reaches. If your stream is quite low, as often occurs during periods of low rainfall some summers, you will probably get better action down low. There are a few streams in the park which may go underground in the lower reaches late in the summer—such as Big Run—so you need to be observant.

There are two aspects about the Hughes that make it special to many anglers.

First, it holds its water level quite well most years thus providing better fishing late in the summer than some of Virginia's mountain streams.

Second, it contains very nice pools and a good population of large trout well up into its headwaters. This provides excellent fishing to those anglers who like to park on the Skyline Drive and hike into the upper reaches of the stream to have it to themselves. It also provides miles of good fishing with dozens of beautiful areas to camp for those who want to backpack into the remote part of the stream and spend several days.

Brokenback Run is a major feeder of the Hughes River which it enters from the south close to the parking lot on the lower end of the Nicholson Hollow trail. This is an excellent trout stream in its own right, falling in size between the Hughes and Hannah. There is excellent water from where it enters the Hughes on upstream well beyond the bridge, and there is no way you can do justice to the whole stream even in a long day of fishing.

The top of the Hughes River can be reached by two different trails off Skyline Drive.

The Corbin Cabin Cutoff Trail provides good access if

The Hughes River is one of the most popular streams in the Park, having good access from the Skyline Drive and the lower valley.

you park at the Shaver Hollow parking area just north of Milepost 38. This trail meets the Nicholson Hollow Trail 1.4 miles down the mountain. The latter trail parallels the stream to the lower park boundary.

You can also park at Stony Man Overlook between Milepost 38 and 39. About 100 yards north is the head of the Nicholson Hollow Trail. Follow this 1.8 miles down to the stream. This is the easiest trail back out.

There is also access at the lower park boundary. Take Route 600 from Nethers past the bus parking lot for Old Rag Mountain. About a half mile on the right is a small parking area. Take the Nicholson Hollow Trail up into the Park.

Access to Brokenback Run is best from the lower park boundary by coming in Route 600. Park either at the upper Old Rag parking area or pull off beside the Nicholson Hollow Trail. The Weakley Hollow Fire Road follows the stream up to the Corbin Hollow Trail, which parallels the stream in the upper section.

Knowledgeable anglers make good catches on the Hughes River and each trout is a joy.

Brokenback Run which runs from the Old Rag ridges into the Hughes River fishes quite well in cold weather.

Hannah Run is easy to reach by parking at the Nicholson Hollow Trail parking area on Route 600 and hiking up Nicholson Hollow Trail 1.9 miles along the Hughes River to where Hannah Run enters the Hughes River from the north.

All three of these streams can be found on the central section map of the Shenandoah National Park.

The Shenandoah National Park collects an entry fee at the lower end of the Hughes River as they do to enter the Skyline Drive.

Chapter 9
White Oak Canyon Run

If one made a list of everything desirable in a mountain free-stone stream and then assembled these in perfect order, the resulting trout stream could easily be White Oak Canyon Run.

There are large brook trout throughout its entire drainage, even in the upper headwaters. In fact, one of my students recently caught the largest wild brookie he'd ever seen in the upper reaches of White Oak Canyon Run.

Whether you are fishing, taking photographs or painting there are numerous incredibly beautiful waterfalls on this stream that will provide you with more than you ever expected.

From an angler's point of view, one of the greatest aspects of this stream is that it provides exceptionally good action from March until December. There are excellent hatches of Quill Gordons and March Browns during the spring. Little Yellow Stoneflies dance across the stream well into July, there are terrestrials galore all summer and Brown Caddis in September to fatten the trout up for their spawning in October.

Early in spring the trout in White Oak Canyon Run take nymphs very well even when the banks are covered with snow.

And, if you have never witnessed the courtship and spawning of wild brook trout in a mountain stream when the canopy of brilliantly colored foliage over the stream challenges the bright colors of the mature trout, you are in for a show. It is not at all unusual to watch four or five pair of trout in a single long pool as the female works to sweep out the bed for her eggs as here large male mate defiantly chases away any smaller would-be partners.

The high-gradient and waterfalls of this stream in the spring present some special angling challenges and provide some subtle blessings.

For example, one day in April I was getting good action on dry flies in the small pools and runs, but when I came to the deeper pools in the steeper parts of the stream the fish seemed not to be looking up. Surprisingly few trout were back on the tails of the pools or in the eddies on the sides of the pools even though there were a fair number of duns on the surface. When I went to nymphs in these deep pools I did quite well. However, try as I might in one deep pool after another it was nymphs or nothing, even though the trout in the runs separating the pools were taking my drys like it was feeding time at the zoo. The trout just insisted that I play by their rules.

These same high-gradient areas are a real blessing in periods of low water in an entirely different way. Frequently late in the summer some of the Park's streams become very low from lack of rain and the trout are very wary. Just simply getting close enough to these trout to make a presentation in the long flat pools is almost impossible. This is where the steep, high-gradient pools in White Oak Canyon Run can save the day.

There are two things working in our favor in these pools which help us greatly. First, the steep nature of the terrain allows us to stay well below the pools as we approach them from below, and we are not as likely to spook the trout as we move in to fish the pools. Secondly, many of these pools are surprisingly deep up close to the heads of the pools, thus apparently giving the trout a degree of comfort they don't find in the shallower, more open pools.

As you can see, it is important to play the water types properly in these mountain streams in order to achieve consistent success.

Cedar Run is the main feeder stream of White Oak Canyon Run and is an excellent brook trout stream in its own right. If you call White Oak a "steep" mountain stream then you would probably call Cedar Run "extremely steep." One particular characteristic of Cedar Run jumps out at you as you look at it on a topo map. Most of the streams in the park take a curved or even zigzag course as they descend from the tops of the mountains to the valleys below. Not Cedar Run! It goes straight down the mountain, so you know it has to be steep.

Most maps show two or three sets of falls on Cedar Run, but actually I think of it as almost a continuous series of mini-waterfalls once you get about a mile up the mountain.

There is a good trail along the stream but I should caution you to keep a keen eye out for the first ford coming in from the bottom. This crosses from the north side of the stream to the south over solid rock ledges and it is very easy to miss—as I did on my first trip. If you find yourself teetering along the side of some very steep cliffs on the north side of the stream wondering where the trial is don't panic. Just go back downstream

Some of the largest brook trout in the Park are found in White Oak Canyon Run.

several hundred yards and you'll see where you missed it.

The deep pools formed by the many steep areas hold some surprisingly large trout for the size of the stream.

A tactic we often use is for one person to fish up White Oak Canyon and one fish up Cedar Run. They are both excellent streams and you should get great action.

White Oak Canyon Run Access

The top access is by parking at Limberlost, just east of the Skyline Drive at Milepost 43. Hike 0.1 mile down Old Rag Fire Road to White Oak Canyon Trail. Follow this trail to the right and it takes you down to the stream, providing good stream access all the way to the bottom of the mountain.

Route 600 provides good access to the lower part of the stream. Park in the area beside the stream and follow White Oak Canyon trail up along the stream.

Cedar Run Access

The lower park boundary provides the best access to this stream. Route 600 leads to the upper parking area. Take the White Oak Trail 0.1 mile west to the Cedar Run Trail which is the first trail to the left after crossing the metal bridge. This trail follows the stream.

Both White Oak Canyon Run and Cedar Run can be found on the central section map of the Shenandoah National Park.

The Shenandoah National Park collects any entry fee at the lower parking area of these streams as they do on the Skyline Drive.

Cedar Run which feeds the lower portion of White Oak Canyon Run gives excellent trout fishing in the spring.

Chapter 10
Rose River

The Rose River is one of the most popular streams in the Park and it is well deserving of this fondness by anglers. It has excellent hatches of Quill Gordons, March Browns, Light-Cahills and Little Yellow Stoneflies which provide outstanding fishing for rising trout from March until June.

However, my favorite time to fish the Rose River is during the summer. Admittedly, the hatches of aquatic insects have thinned out greatly, but Nature has more than compensated the trout for this by supplying an abundance of terrestrial insects from the thick tree canopy which shades the stream.

There is a profusion of ants, beetles and other landborne insects which the trout gorge upon. One insect referred to locally as a "mountain wasp" appears to be a real favorite of the trout for when these are on the water they never pass them up. Drifting a size 16 Shenk's Cricket over one of these wasp-feeders is about as surefire as trout fishing gets. They seldom let it drift by.

Much of the infatuation the Park's streams hold in the summer is the opportunity to go one on one with individual trout. Few serious anglers kill any trout in these streams so even in the summer there is still an excellent population present. And the Rose, having a larger than normal water level, has a good population of large trout.

As I approach each pool in the summer I stay well below it and carefully observe every possible feeding station in order to see if I can spot several trout or their rise forms. In most cases if there is good light it takes less than a minute to see several trout. Next I plot my strategy of exactly how I should approach the pool and where I should deliver my first cast in order to take the desired fish first then move on to the next.

The Rose River offers the angler spectacular waterfalls as well as excellent brook trout fishing.

Anglers who are willing to hike into the remote parts of the Rose River find outstanding fishing and beautiful scenery.

When everything goes according to plan this ploy usually works. But then, I can see clearly in my mind's eye the beautiful pool with its seven rising trout many years ago that I observed and photographed for about fifteen minutes. After I had gotten about a dozen photographs I carefully plotted my route of approach in order to fish the pool effectively. You're right, I spooked all seven as I moved in before I even got a chance to make a cast.

My most effective summer flies on the Rose River, as well as other mountain streams in Virginia, are Ed Shenk's Cricket in size 16, Black and Cinnamon Ants in sizes 16, 18, 20 and 22 and Beetles in sizes 16, 18, and 20.

Obviously the low-floating Beetles and Ants can be difficult for us to see in these heavily shaded mountain hollows so over the years we've made alterations to these patterns to enhance their angler visibility which helps greatly. My son Jeff suggested transplanting a yellow wing from our popular Mr. Rapidan dry fly to the Black Ant, tying as a parachute and calling it the Mr. Rapidan Ant. To help see the Crowe Beetle on the water we added a short upward-sloping light elk-hair wing and named it Murray's Flying Beetle. These patterns are much easier for us to see than their predecessors and trout take them just as readily.

Little refinements like this certainly simplify our angling game.

In order to help achieve the delicate, accurate presentations needed in the low, clear streams of summer we use two- and three-weight rods and nine-foot leaders tapered down to 6X on the size 16 and 18 flies and go to 7X if needed with size 20, 22 and 24 flies.

About three miles up the stream from the lower park boundary Hog Camp Branch comes in from the south. This contributes about two-thirds of the water volume of the Rose River but the north branch (technically still the Rose River) carries a good water volume, and I've had many wonderful days fishing it.

There is a beautiful waterfall on this upper part of the Rose River that can be a little intimidating the first time you fish this area.

One tends to fish up the stream, paying more attention to the pools and fish before him than to the waterfalls ahead. Then as you complete fishing the two beautiful pools immediately below the falls and prepare to head on up the stream you realize you are boxed into a deep canyon with very steep, high walls on both sides and no way out except to walk back down the stream to more friendly terrain. I remember the first time I found myself up under these falls with each sidewall little more than a rod's length away with overhanging ledges on the tops of the cliffs. I thought, "These rock cliffs must have been like this for thousands of years, now if they will just stay put for another fifteen minutes I can get back out of here."

Hog Camp Branch is a good small stream with about a mile of nice water. The gradient is very steep with many large sloping ledges so one needs to use extra caution when climbing from pool to pool. The hatches, season and tactics for this branch are the same as they are for the Rose River. However, with less water volume than the lower part of the Rose River the trout become very wary late in the summer in a dry year.

Rose River Access

Top access is available from the Skyline Drive by parking at the Fishers Gap parking area just south of Milepost 49 and hiking down the Rose River Fire Road, which follows the lower two-thirds of the stream to the lower park boundary. An alternate trail to the uppermost part of the river is available by parking at the above area, but shortly after starting down the mountain on the Rose River Fire Road take the Rose River Loop Trail to your left. The first 0.5 mile of this trail is blazed yellow since it also functions as a horse trail. One half mile down the trail take a blue-blazed trail to your right for another 0.5 mile to the stream.

The Hogcamp Branch of the Rose River is one of its two main branches and they both hold good populations of brook trout.

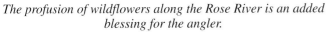

The profusion of wildflowers along the Rose River is an added blessing for the angler.

Top access can also be gained by parking at the Dark Hollow Falls parking area and following the Dark Hollow Falls Trail down to the Rose River Fire Road and then following the fire road down to the river. This road has many cut backs, and in some areas it is far from the stream. In these areas there is no good trail close to the stream. You keep your bearings by knowing the road is "up there somewhere" and that the stream is "down there somewhere."

Hogcamp Branch Access

The quickest access to this stream is by parking at Dark Hollow Falls parking area. This is located between Milepost 50 and 51 on the eastern side of the drive. Hiking down the Dark Hollow Falls Trail puts you right on the stream.

An alternate approach is from the parking area at Fisher Gap just south of Milepost 49. Hike down the Rose River Fire Road until you cross the stream. Just across the stream the trail leaves the fire road and follows the stream down to where it joins the Rose River—about a mile.

Both of these streams are on the central section map of the Shenandoah National Park.

Chapter 11
Rapidan River

The Mr. Rapidan Dry Fly which the author developed and named for the Rapidan River is one of the most productive dry flies in Virginia's trout streams.

The one aspect about this stream which has always made it very special to me is that President Herbert Hoover had his fishing camp here while he served in the White House.

His directions to his secretary Lawrence Ritchey are quite interesting: "Find a summer-camp on a trout stream within 100 miles of Washington, at an elevation of 2,500 feet or more so as to be away from mosquito-breeding waters and have a climate affording relief from the capital city's exhausting heat."

Actually these criteria sound as rewarding to us today as they were for President Hoover in 1929. And as we look at some of the President's statements we can easily see that trout fishing was as important to him as it is to us.

He told his personal physician Dr. Joel T. Boone that, "Fishing is a constant reminder of the democracy of life, of humility and of human frailty—for all men are equal before fishes," and that "everybody considers that fish will not bite in the presence of the public."

In a more formal statement when he addressed the Izaak Walton League he stated, "Man and boy, the American is a fisherman. That comprehensive list of human rights, the Declaration of Independence, is firm that all men (and boys) are endowed with

certain inalienable rights, including life, liberty, and the pursuit of happiness, which obviously includes the pursuit of fish....."

This makes sense to me, so when he felt the Rapidan River was a good place to fish that was good enough for me.

If you would like to see Camp Hoover you can park at Milam Gap on the Skyline Drive and hike about two miles down the Mill Prong Trail. Or you can come in the bottom of the mountain on Route 649/670 past Criglersville, drive to the end of the road, park and walk about a mile and half up the fire road to Camp Hoover. This road can be very rough at times so you may prefer the access from Skyline Drive.

The tactics and fly patterns for the Rapidan River are much the same as they are for other park streams. However, I did hit a situation one spring which you may want to take advantage of if you hit similar conditions.

Late-spring rains had caused the stream to rise and become slightly discolored. The normal tactics with drys, regular nymphs and even weighted nymphs had failed to produce any trout at all. More out of frustration than from any well-conceived plan I put on a size 10 Black Shenk's Sculpin Streamer and started searching out the deep protected areas beneath overhanging boulders and ledges. Right away I began to pick up one nice brook trout after another.

The next time I hit the stream in a similar condition I used the same tactics and had excellent fishing. I've experimented with other streamers under these full-stream conditions in the park and I've found the size 10 Black Strymph is equally as good as the Sculpin.

Like the Rose, Hughes and White Oak Canyon Run, the Rapidan River holds up well during the summer and provides good fishing.

The Staunton River enters the Rapidan from the south in the lower part of the stream. This is a nice small stream, but recent floods have caused damage in the lower section. You need to hike up above the falls to get good fishing.

Route 649/670 from Criglersville provides good access to the central part of the Rapidan River.

Route 662 via Graves Mills provides good access to the lower part of the Rapidan River and to the Staunton River.

The Rapidan and Staunton rivers can be found on the central section of the Shenandoah National Park Maps.

The Staunton River, which is a small feeder stream to the Rapidan River, gives good action in the spring.

The Rapidan River is well known because President Herbert Hoover had a camp here while he was president.

Chapter 12
Conway River

The Conway River is one of the prettiest streams in the Blue Ridge Mountains. In late April the sides of the streams and trails are covered with trillium, jack in the pulpit and other wildflowers while the ridges are painted with the blooms of red bud and dogwood trees. This is also prime time for the trout fishing on this stream if you want to hit good hatches of aquatic insects.

From the middle of April until the middle of May the hatches of the Dark Blue Quills, March Browns, Gray Fox, Light Cahills and Little Yellow Stoneflies overlap, and it is not at all unusual to see several trout in each pool feeding on them all indiscriminately. However, one needs to be alert to the whims of the trout for they may change the game and become very demanding as they did for me one cold day in April several years ago.

The Dark Blue Quill hatch had been on for about a week and they were about at their peak of concentration during a year of an unusually large abundance of these insects. The

Good hatches of March Brown mayflies bring many of the trout to the surface providing good dry-fly fishing.

trout had become accustomed to feeding actively on the duns drifting naturally along the currents as they prepared to fly from the stream. Suddenly the weather changed; the air

The Conway River is a nice stream to fish in the spring while the water level is good.

The Devil's Ditch, the major feeder of the Conway River, starts off gently but quickly becomes very steep and rugged showing why the early settlers gave it this name.

temperature dropped drastically and there were snow flurries in the mountains for several days.

The delicate little Dark Blue Quill mayflies continued to attempt to hatch, but apparently the cold air temperature prevented them from making their normal, fast getaways from the stream's surface. The currents forced many of them to the sides of the pools, and the back eddies held dozens of these struggling mayflies, many still partly trapped in their nymph shucks. Watching the little flotillas of drifting insects and foam was quite an education, for many of the flies would drift around the back eddies three or four times before they would fly away. Obviously these lazily floating tidbits and gentle currents created perfect feeding stations for the trout, and each eddy held several large trout gently sipping in the naturals.

I thought it looked like a perfect situation to easily take many large trout on drys. However, as my size 16 dry Dark Blue Quill failed to bring a single strike in one back eddy after another, I decided to investigate. Leaving my fly rod and vest behind, I cautiously crawled in beside one of the eddies to see just what the trout were doing. Lying there on my stomach I could hardly believe my eyes. The trout were selectively feeding on only those mayflies which were still struggling to free themselves from their nymph shuck. After watching this for a long time I slithered back away from the stream and retrieved my rod and vest. Replacing my dry with an emerger and dressing both the leader and the fly with silicone cream was the answer, for I was able to fool many nice trout with this rig for the next several days.

My point here is that we need to be observant of what the trout are doing at all times and adapt our tactics accordingly.

On the average year the Conway River holds up well until July, but late July and August can produce low-water conditions and very wary trout.

There is about a five-mile stretch of good water upstream of the parking area at the end of Route 667 above Fletcher and about two miles of good water on the Devil's Ditch.

The Devil's Ditch is the main feeder stream of the Conway River, entering the south side of the stream in the lower area about a mile above the lower parking area on Route 667. The Devil's Ditch in a good brook trout stream. It has a very steep gradient and is quite rugged with steep cliffs stabbing skyward in many areas.

As you fish up this stream in the deep part of the canyon, it takes little imagination to envision how the early settlers came up with the name "Devil's Ditch." Actually the steep nature of this stream is what makes it as good as it is. For with only a moderate flow many surprisingly deep pools are formed that provide perfect habitat for the brook trout. By sneaking in below the tails of these pools it is an easy matter to remain hidden and cast a dry fly just a few feet upstream to take a trout or two from each pool.

The Conway flows in and out of the park, but since the state portion is managed the same as the park's streams, I'm including it here.

Route 667 through Fletcher is the main access. Drive up to the end of the road and park on the north side of the stream where you will not block traffic or interfere with private land owners.

The Old Conway River Road follows the stream for its full length providing easy hiking access.

The alternate way into the Conway is by Route 662 and 615 across a sometimes very rough road. Going in is not too bad, but one wet spring day I was very concerned about getting back up that mountain road. This road hits the stream only a short distance above where you can reach it via 667 so you really don't gain much.

Both the Conway River and the Devil's Ditch can be found on the Central Section of the Shenandoah National Park Map.

The hollows which feed the Conway River have extremely thick areas of dogwood, red bud and a dense growth of many wildflowers.

Chapter 13
Big Run

This is one of the finest streams in the park and I've always taken more big trout here than on the other streams.

Two factors contribute to the size of these brookies. There are numerous very large, deep pools which provide good protection for the trout and many of the hatches of aquatic insects are very heavy.

These two factors bring about one of my favorite ways to fish Big Run. When the hatches of some of our largest mayflies, such as the Quill Gordons and March Browns, are at their peak in the evenings with duns coming off and spinners returning to the streams to mate and lay eggs, I like to observe these big pools and find the largest feeder. Once I've located my trout I carefully move into casting position—sometimes on my hands and knees. Once I'm in position I watch my trout feed for a few minutes. This is more for my benefit than his, for it lets me calm my nerves and fine-tune my strategy. When I've pinpointed the trout's feeding station by his rise forms, I shoot my dry fly about two feet above him onto a current that will drift it naturally to him.

Sometimes I fool these big surface feeders and sometime they are too smart for me, but I find this one on one game very gratifying.

Big Run has one of the longest drainages in the park. And if you add to this the length of its two main feeders Rocky Mountain Run and Eppert Hollow Run there is more water than you can do justice to in a week of fishing. I've always enjoyed fishing Rocky Mountain Run especially down low where it enters Big Run.

Even though Big Run is one of the largest streams in the park with a great flow in the spring it often gets very low late in the summer. I've seen the lower part of the stream with only a trickle of water between the pools with the trout locked into the pools. However, several miles up the mountain the flow picks up and the stream is fishable.

This really does not present a problem because there is no legal access at the lower part of the stream.

Big Run lying in a very steep, long hollow is one of the Park's best trout streams.
The outstanding fishing is worth the long hike.

The great population of wild brook trout and its remote location make Big Run an ideal stream on which to camp and fish for several days.

There are two trails into Big Run from the Skyline Drive. The easiest access, although the pull is far from easy, is to park at Doyles River Parking on the east side of the Skyline Drive just south of Milepost 81. From the Big Run Overlook take the Big Run Loop Trail, which connects with the Big Run Portal Trail 2.2 miles down the mountain. The stream is quite small here so you will probably want to hike down this trail toward Rocky Mountain Run.

The second access point is from Brown Mountain Overlook at Milepost 77. Take the Brown Mountain Trail down 0.7 miles to the Rocky Mountain Run Trail, and follow this 2.7 miles down to Big Run. The upper section of this trail is very steep, making a long, tough pull back after fishing all day.

Fishing Big Run should definitely be looked on as a rugged wilderness trek, not to be attempted with little thought, or if you are not in good physical condition. Consider packing in to make the best use of your time and to break up the hike.

Big Run can be found on the southern section of the Shenandoah National Park map.

Many of the deep, fast pools in Big Run hold some surprisingly large trout.

Chapter 14

Shenandoah National Park Facilities And Information

OVERNIGHT ACCOMMODATIONS:

Skyland
Dining room, tap room, conference hall, crafts, horseback riding, children's playground, religious service provided by a Christian ministry, naturalist activities (include conducted hikes and evening programs).
   Season: Late March through October
   Mile: 41.7
   Phone: Information & Reservation 800-999-4714 during season months; during December through March call (540)743-5108.

Big Meadows Lodge
Dining room, tap room, craft shop, children's playground, religious services provided by a Christian ministry, naturalist activities (include conducted hikes and evening programs).
   Season: Mid-May through October
   Mile: 51.3; one mile off Drive
   Phone: Information & Reservation 800-999-4714

Lewis Mountain Cabins
Cottages (furnished with bathroom, lights, heat, towels, and linen), camp store, laundry, showers, wood, ice.
   Season: May through October
   Mile: 57.6
   Phone: Information & Reservation 800-999-4714

Information for above lodges:
• Check-out time is 12:00 noon.
• Check-in time is approximately 3:00 p.m.
• No pets are allowed in the overnight accommodations.
• There are no phones in any rooms. A limited number of rooms have television. Public phones and TV lounges are available at Skyland and Big Meadows Lodge.
• For reservations, you may also write ARAMARK, P.O. Box 727, Luray, VA 22835. 1-800-999-4714 or (540) 743-5108.

DINING:

Panorama Restaurant
Dining room, gift and craft shop
   Season: May through October
   Mile: 31.5

Skyland Restaurant
Serves breakfast, lunch and dinner
   Season: April through October
   Mile: 41.7

Big Meadows Lodge Restaurant
Serves breakfast, lunch and dinner
   Season: Mid-May through October
   Mile: 51.3; one mile off Drive

VISITOR CENTERS:

Dickey Ridge Visitor Center
This attractive building was converted from an abandoned lodge in 1958. Exhibits introduce what you can see and do in the park. Rangers are available to give short talks on the area's history and natural history.
   Season: From about April 1 through November 1.
   Info (540) 635-3566.
   Mile: 4.6

Byrd Visitor Center
This facility was built in 1966 and named for Senator Harry F. Byrd, Sr. It contains exhibits on the people and natural history of Shenandoah National Park and Big Meadows. Ranger-led hikes and programs are offered during spring, summer, and fall; a free movie is shown regularly. General information (540) 999-3283.
   Season: Open daily from early Memorial Day week and through late fall.
   Mile: 51

CAMPGROUNDS:
The park has four rustic campgrounds with no hookups for electricity, sewage, or water. There's a 14-day total limit between June 1 and October 31. Check headquarters (540) 999-3500 for opening and closing dates.

Mathews Arm Campground
179 tent and trailer sites, sewage disposal station, summer walks, and evening programs offered by rangers (consult campground bulletin boards for times and locations), Traces Nature Trail, no shower facilities.
   Nearby: 2 miles from Elkwallow Wayside & Campstore.
   Mile: 22.2

Big Meadows Campground
217 sites, reservations through Biospheries Inc., May through October, wood, ice, showers, laundry facilities, amphitheater programs, sewage disposal. Nearby: Big Meadows Lodge & Wayside, gas, picnic area, Byrd Visitor Center, Story of the Forest Trail, Ranger-led activities and programs in spring, summer and fall. (Check park bulletin boards for times and locations.) For reservations call 1-800-365-CAMP. For information call (540) 999-3500.
   Milepost: 51

Lewis Mountain Campground
32 campsites, picnic area, camp store, showers, laundry facilities, rustic cabins
   Mile: 57.5

Loft Mountain Campground
219 campsites, showers, laundry facilities, Loft Mountain Information Center, Loft Mountain Wayside and camp store, Deadening Nature Trail, sewage disposal, Ranger activities, and amphitheater programs. (Summer, check park bulletin boards for times and locations.)
   Mile: 79.5

EMERGENCIES
If you need help or first aid, want to report a missing person, or have any emergency of any kind, contact the nearest Ranger at any visitor center, campground, entrance station, or Ranger Station. You could also send another driver hiker to find a Ranger, ask concession personnel at waysides or lodges to contact a Ranger for you, or call the emergency Phone: numbers at headquarters, staffed 24 hours a day: 1-800-732-0911. Pay phones are located in developed areas.

FISHING LICENSE
A State of Virginia license is required. A five-day license is available at wayside facilities and camp stores in the park. Since the fishing regulations can change, get a current copy when you purchase your license.

Outside the Park Eastern Side of the Shenandoah National Park
(North to South)

FRONT ROYAL, VIRGINIA

Motels/Hotels:
Quality Inn Skyline Drive
10 Commerce Ave.
Front Royal, VA 22630
   Phone: (540) 635-3161 or 800-821-4488
• Located near north entrance to Skyline Drive, 552 Bypass.
• 107 rooms, dining room, swimming pool.

Pioneer Motel
541 S. Royal Ave.
Front Royal, VA 22630
   Phone: (540) 635-4784
• Located on US 340 near Skyline Drive and caverns. 28 rooms, pool, A/C, cable color TV w/HBO, refrigerator, oversized beds available, restaurant, and gift shop.

BED & BREAKFAST INNS:
The Woodward House on Manor Grade Bed & Breakfast
   413 S. Royal Ave.
   Front Royal, VA 22630
   Phone: (540) 635-7010 & 1-800-635-7011
• Located at intersection of Rt. 340 and Rt. 55. Three blocks to north entrance to Skyline Drive and Shenandoah National Park.
• 6 double rooms with private bath and 3 suites with private bath, fireplaces, game room.

CAMPGROUNDS:
Front Royal KOA
P.O. Box 274
Front Royal, VA 22630
Phone: (540) 635-2741 or 1-800-KOA-9114

WASHINGTON, VIRGINIA

Bed & Breakfast Inns
   Inn at Little Washington
   P.O. Box 300
   Washington, VA 22747
Phone: (540) 675-3800
• Rates are expensive, includes full breakfast. Open all year. 8 rooms and 2 penthouse suites with Jacuzzi; restaurant open Wed. through Sun. Dinner only, for guests and public. Children over ten; no pets.

Foster-Harris House
P.O. Box 333
189 Main St.
Washington, VA 22747
Phone: (540) 675-3757 or 1-800-666-0153

SYRIA, VIRGINIA

BED & BREAKFAST INNS
Grave's Mountain Lodge
Rt. 670
Syria, VA 22743
Phone: (540) 923-4231

CULPEPER, VIRGINIA

MOTELS/HOTELS

Holiday Inn
P.O. Box 1206
Culpeper, VA 22701
Phone: (540) 825-1253 or 800-HOLIDAY
• Located on Rt. 29 South

Comfort Inn
890 Willis Ln.
Culpeper, VA 22701
Phone: (540) 825-4900 or 1-800-228-5150

CAMPGROUNDS

Cedar Mountain Campground
Culpeper, VA 22701
Phone: (540) 547-3374 or 1-800-234-0968
• Located 25 miles from Skyline Drive. From Rt. 29/15 turn east on Rt. 603, right on 657, right on 645, left on 752.
• Tent/trailer sites (woods or field), tables, fireplace, dumping station, water and electric hookups, field for primitive camping, toilets, and hot showers.

MADISON, VIRGINIA

BED & BREAKFAST INNS

Dulaney Hollow Guesthouse
Rt. 231
Madison, VA 22727
Phone: (540) 923-4470

CAMPGROUNDS

Shenandoah Hills Campground
Rt. 1, Box 7
Madison, VA 22727
Phone: (540) 948-4186
• Located at the foot of the Blue Ridge Mountains and the Shenandoah National Park on Rt. 29 South, 2 miles south of town of Madison.
• 89 sites, electric, sewer, nature trails, recreation building, store, playground, swimming, dump station, LP gas, pets on leash, laundry. Open March 15 until November 15, reservations accepted.

WESTERN SIDE OF THE SHENANDOAH NATIONAL PARK (NORTH TO SOUTH)

EDINBURG, VIRGINIA (AREA)

Motel

Budget Host Inn
1290 S. Main St.
Woodstock, VA 22664
Phone: (540) 459-4086

FLY SHOP

Murray's Fly Shop
P.O. Box 156
121 Main St.
Edinburg, VA 22824
Phone: (540) 984-4212
Fax: (540) 984-4895
E-mail: murrays@shentel.net
Web: www.murraysflyshop.com
• This is a complete fly shop, providing all tackle needs by Scott, Winston, Orvis, Sage, Loomis and Hardy.
• Over 50,000 trout, bass and saltwater flies in stock.
• Complete fly shop, schools for both bass and trout
• Guide service for bass and trout (tackle provided free)
• Free mail-order catalog
• Maps of trout and bass streams

LURAY, VIRGINIA

MOTELS/HOTELS

Ramada Inn
138 Whispering Hill Rd.
Luray, VA 22835
Phone: (540) 743-4521

The Mimslyn Inn
401 W. Main St.
Luray, VA 22835
Phone: (540) 743-5105 or 1-800-296-5105
• Elegant surroundings, fine food, conference facilities, lounge.

CAMPGROUNDS

Yogi Bear Jellystone Camp Resort
Luray, VA 22835
Phone: (540) 743-4002
Located 5 miles west of Skyline Drive on US 211.
• 150 sites, water, electric, sewer hookups, sewage dump station, showers, laundry facilities, firewood for sale, store, playground, game room, pool, fishing. Open Mar.-Oct.

STANLEY, VIRGINIA

BED & BREAKFAST INNS

Jordan Hollow Farm Inn
P.O. Box 375
326 Hawkbill Park Rd.
Stanley, VA 22851
Phone: (540) 778-2209 or (540) 778-2285
• Located about 8 miles from Luray. From Rt. 340, 6 miles south, turn left onto 624, left on Rt. 689, and right on Rt. 626. 20 rooms with private bath, no pets allowed.

ELKTON, VIRGINIA

Motels/Hotels

Elkton Motel
Elkton, VA 22827
Phone: (540) 298-1463
• Located on US 33 east.

BED & BREAKFAST INN

Jo Ann's Bed & Breakfast
4629 Bloomer Spring Rd.
Elkton, VA 22827
Phone: (540) 298-9723
• Located on Rt. 33 east on a farm 3 miles from Massanutten.
• Full breakfast, private bath, and entrance.

CAMPGROUNDS

Swift Run Campground
19540 Spotswood Trail
Elkton, VA 22827
Phone: (540) 298-8086
• Located 4 miles west of Skyline Drive on US 33.
• 40 sites, water, electric, sewer hookups, sewage dump station, showers, laundry facilities, firewood for sale, store, game room, pool. Open all year.

WAYNESBORO, VIRGINIA

MOTELS/HOTELS

Comfort Inn
640 W. Broad St.
Waynesboro, VA 22980
Phone: 800-228-5150 or (540) 942-1171
• Located near entrance to Skyline Drive and Blue Ridge Parkway. 2.9 miles north of I-64, Exit 96 and 3 miles west I-64, Main St. on Rt. 250-340 bypass.
• 75 rooms, A/C, pool, cable TV, attractive guest rooms. Restaurant adjacent with 10% discount for all guest meals, children under 16 free.

Holiday Inn-Afton Mountain
P.O. Box 549
Rt. 250 I-64
Waynesboro VA 22980
Phone: (540) 942-5201
• Located 5 miles east of Waynesboro, where Skyline Drive meets the Blue Ridge Parkway. I-64, Exit 99.

CAMPGROUNDS

Waynesboro Campground
Rt. 3 Box 333
Waynesboro VA
Phone: (540) 943-9573
• Located 6 miles north of Waynesboro on US 340.
• 130 sites, water and electric hookups, sewage dump station, showers, laundry facilities, store, game room, pool.

FOR ADDITIONAL INFORMATION:

Shenandoah National Park, Skyline Drive
3655 US Hwy. 211 E
Luray, VA 22835
Phone: (540) 999-3500 for Emergencies Only
1-800-732-0911

The Shenandoah Natural History Association
Shenandoah National Park
3655 US Hwy. 211 E
Luray, VA 22835
Phone: (540) 999-3582

Shenandoah Valley Travel Association
277 W. Old Cross Rd.
New Market, VA 22844
Phone: (540) 740-3132

Murray's Fly Shop
P.O. Box 156
Edinburg, VA 22824
Phone: (540) 984-4212
E-mail: murrays@shentel.net
Web: www.murraysflyshop.com
• PATC Maps and fishing information.

DRY FLIES

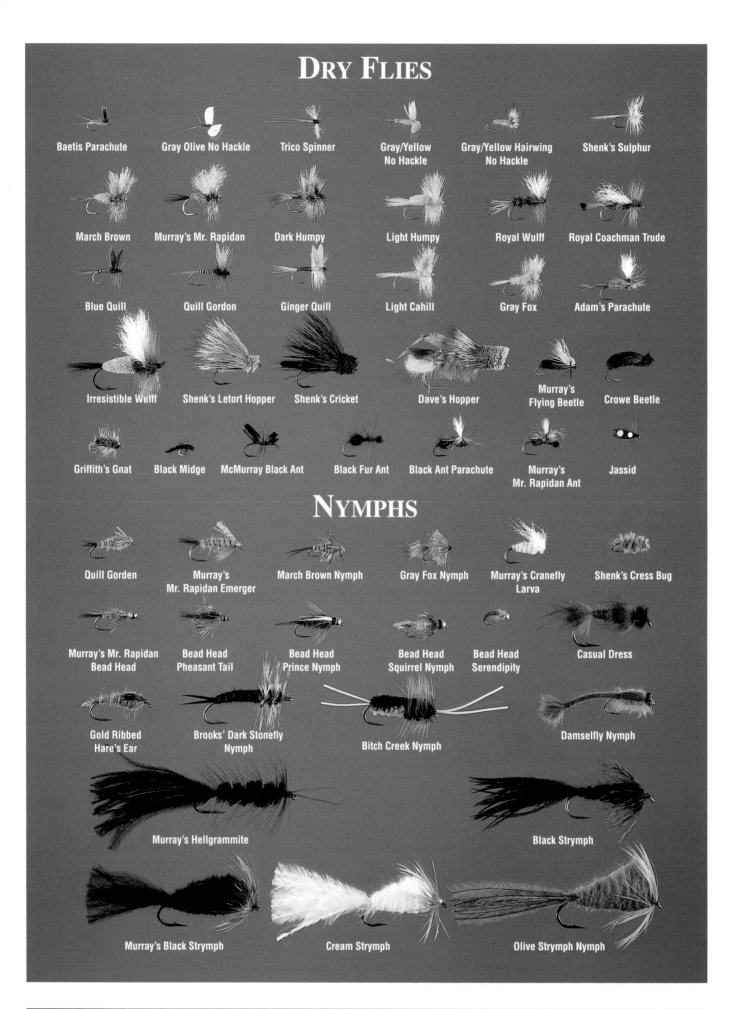

Baetis Parachute   Gray Olive No Hackle   Trico Spinner   Gray/Yellow No Hackle   Gray/Yellow Hairwing No Hackle   Shenk's Sulphur

March Brown   Murray's Mr. Rapidan   Dark Humpy   Light Humpy   Royal Wulff   Royal Coachman Trude

Blue Quill   Quill Gordon   Ginger Quill   Light Cahill   Gray Fox   Adam's Parachute

Irresistible Wulff   Shenk's Letort Hopper   Shenk's Cricket   Dave's Hopper   Murray's Flying Beetle   Crowe Beetle

Griffith's Gnat   Black Midge   McMurray Black Ant   Black Fur Ant   Black Ant Parachute   Murray's Mr. Rapidan Ant   Jassid

NYMPHS

Quill Gorden   Murray's Mr. Rapidan Emerger   March Brown Nymph   Gray Fox Nymph   Murray's Cranefly Larva   Shenk's Cress Bug

Murray's Mr. Rapidan Bead Head   Bead Head Pheasant Tail   Bead Head Prince Nymph   Bead Head Squirrel Nymph   Bead Head Serendipity   Casual Dress

Gold Ribbed Hare's Ear   Brooks' Dark Stonefly Nymph   Bitch Creek Nymph   Damselfly Nymph

Murray's Hellgrammite   Black Strymph

Murray's Black Strymph   Cream Strymph   Olive Strymph Nymph

STREAMERS

Olive Woolly Bugger

Black Woolly Bugger

Silver Outcast

Murray's Madtom

Murray's Pearl Marauder

Murray's Black Marauder

Shenk's Black Sculpin

Whitlock Sculpin

Spuddler

White Marabou Muddler

Shenk's White Streamer

Clouser's Deep Sculpin

BASS FLIES

Potomac Popper

Shenandoah Blue Popper

Shenandoah Darter Popper

Shenandoah Damsel Popper

Shenandoah Slider—Chartreuse

Whitlock's Frog

Improved Sofa Pillow

Whitlock's Mouserat

Tapply Deer Hair Bug—Green/White

Chapter 15
Passage Creek

This stream flows through the beautiful Fort Valley just east of Edinburg in Shenandoah and Warren counties.

The upper reaches of Passage Creek originate in the deep shaded, hollows of the Massanutten Mountains. It picks up many rich springs as it flows north through the farms in the valley for about twenty miles. At this point the mountains choke in on each side of the stream causing it to flow faster and drop more rapidly as it tumbles over many huge boulders.

This northernmost part of the stream flows through the George Washington National Forest and then land belonging to the Virginia Commission of Game and Inland Fisheries. There is excellent access here and the fishing is quite good. Special regulations in the northern part of the stream help assure the quality of the fishery.

The Elizabeth Furnace campground and picnic areas are right beside the stream in this northern area. These are well maintained by the Lee District of the George Washington National Forest, providing clean, neat facilities for the angler and his family.

Early in March many anglers do well in size 10 and 12 streamers and size 12 and 14 nymphs. Good hatches of

Passage Creek often holds some very nice sized rainbows.

mayflies begin in mid-March and one can expect to see rising trout in the slower sections of the stream. During the summer crickets, hoppers, beetles and ants will fool the tougher trout.

This downstream section of the stream is accessible from Route 678 which parallels it and Route 619 which crosses it from Route 678 at the fish hatchery.

The extreme upstream part of the stream is accessible from Route 274 through Crisman Hollow by turning off south from Route 675 about a mile west of Camp Roosevelt.

This upper area carries a small water volume which can often give good fishing even if the area around Elizabeth

One can often get good dry-fly fishing in the upper reaches of Passage Creek about the time the red bud blooms in April.

Furnace is too high. I've had many great days in this section in March with standard drys and nymphs. My fishing partners recently hit this section when the cicadas were out...said it was like feeding time at the zoo. Every rainbow in the stream was stuffed with cicadas and looking for more.

For those interested in hiking, the Tuscarora Trail crosses this stream in the Elizabeth Furnace area and continues east to the Shenandoah National Park where it ties into the Appalachian Trail. To the west it leads to Little North Mountain through Fetzers Gap.

As you can see, this is a great vacation area for the whole family. And keep in mind, there is fine smallmouth bass fishing in both the North and South Forks of the Shenandoah River which are just a few miles to the west and east respectfully of Passage Creek. These rivers are covered elsewhere in this book.

Services In This Area

Since this stream is very close to Big Stoney Creek the accommodations are the same as those listed at the end of the discussion on Big Stoney Creek in Shenandoah County.

Chapter 16

Big Stoney Creek and Little Stoney Creek

The delicious wild morel mushroom, which thrives in the Shenandoah Valley in the spring, is sought with enthusiasm equal to that of the trout.

Big Stoney Creek along Route 675 west of Edinburg in Shenandoah County is one of the finest stocked trout streams in Virginia.

There are primarily two factors which contribute to this fishery that make it ideal for both the trout and the angler.

Shenandoah Valley's Big Stoney Creek runs over many miles of rich limestone which has a positive influence upon both the aquatic insects and the trout.

Secondly, the abundance of springs that enter the stream throughout its length cool it during the summer to provide a comfortable environment for the trout, while warming it early in the spring and late in the fall which prompts the trout to feed more aggressively than they would otherwise.

Some of the fastest action takes place from March to June from Lantz Mill on Route 675 upstream through Columbia Furnace and west for the next several miles.

In early March the best fishing is usually with streamers like the Olive Strymph, Black Strymph and Black Woolly Bugger all in size 10 and with nymphs like the Casual Dress, Mr. Rapidan Bead Head and Prince Bead Head in sizes 12 and 14.

By the second week of April, very heavy hatches of mayflies and caddisflies have the trout looking up and it is

Big Stoney Creek west of Edinburg flows through the heart of the Shenandoah Valley where it offers good trout fishing and beautiful scenery.

The rich springs on Big Stoney Creek host good populations of cress bugs and the large browns take the artificial Cress Bug quite well.

possible to get good action with drys such as the Olive Elk Hair Caddis, the Mr. Rapidan Dry and the March Brown Dry all in sizes 14 and 16.

During the summer I go to the sections of the stream below the largest springs, such as those around Lantz Mill. On hot summer days I get great action by crawling into the tail of the long flat pools and fishing a size 20 Black McMurray Ant on a long 6X leader to trout cruising about the pools to feed on natural terrestrials.

There are several miles of excellent spring-fed water just upstream from Columbia Furnace. The stream here is composed of long, flat pools and runs separated by gentle riffles. It is not at all unusual to spot several rising trout in the flat pools during the summer as you drive up the road beside the stream. Of course, there was the time I came to a screeching halt when I spotted these risers and proceeded to spook them all in my haste to get into the stream. I know you will do better.

A short distance upstream Little Stoney Creek, an excellent wild brook trout stream, enters Big Stoney Creek.

Little Stoney Creek originates in the George Washington National Forest high on Great North Mountain.

The most popular access is to turn north off Route 675 onto Forest Service Route 92 about three miles east of the Wolf Gap Recreation Area. Follow Route 92 down the mountain to where it crosses Little Stoney. At this point you can either fish upstream or, as most anglers prefer,

hike down the trail beside the stream and fish back up to the car.

About 1985 stream studies by the Virginia Department of Game and Inland Fisheries on Little Stoney Creek prompted a combined effort with the George Washington National Forest to add limestone to the stream. The results were dramatic. The trouts' growth rates and reproduction success and the density of

The wild trout in Little Stoney Creek feed well on the surface from March until December.

aquatic insects all improved greatly. Utilizing the chemistry department at James Madison University to help monitor the stream, limestone has been added to the stream as needed. The trout population, and thus the anglers, have benefited greatly from these efforts.

Little Stoney Creek produces good fishing from March until November if the water level holds up well. Years in which there is little rain during the summer the stream may become quite low and the trout exceedingly wary. However, conditions usually improve in the fall and one can expect good fishing.

The Woodstock Reservoir is located about two miles downstream from where Forest Service Route 92 crosses Little Stoney Creek. There is an excellent trail all the way down and the hiking is easy. To take advantage of some unusual fishing for Virginia you can carry a float tube down to the reservoir and launch it at the upper end and fish for cruising wild brook trout throughout the reservoir.

A very enjoyable tactic is to fish the tree-line areas with small dry flies. You can go one on one with rising trout or you can just fish the productive-looking areas.

An alternative tactic is to search out the deeper water with small streamers such as a size 10 Black Strymph or a size 12 Olive Woolly Bugger. In the deepest water a fast sinking-tip fly line can help you get your flies to the bottom.

The stream and road below the dam go through private land and this area is not open to public fishing.

A kick boat is the ideal way to fish for cruising brook trout on the reservoir on Little Stoney Creek west of Edinburg.

Chapter 17
Bullpasture River

The Bullpasture River is located in one of the most beautiful parts of Virginia. And the "Gorge" section of this stream adjacent to the Highland State Wildlife Management Area, upstream from the village of Williamsville, is definitely one of the most scenic areas on the East Coast.

Fortunately, for the angler, Bullpasture River flows through this gorge and offers a variety of trout fishing to meet the whims of the most demanding anglers.

For example, the first time I fished this stream was in the sixties when we had a Trout Unlimited State Council meeting in a private cabin at Williamsville. It was early April and the stream was carrying a great amount of water even though it was clear and fishable. The friend I was fishing with, who knew the stream well, told me there were some large browns in the stream but that they were difficult to take.

Since the Bullpasture was carrying about the same amount of water as one of my favorite streams in Montana which always produced some nice browns to huge Sculpin Streamers I decided to use some of these flies.

My friend, who had never seen anyone use streamers this large for trout, was obviously shocked by my selection. His disapproval was obvious as he inspected my huge Black Sculpin Streamer, he cringed and stated, " I didn't know it was legal to use young alligators as trout bait." I didn't say a word at the end of the day when it turned out that this was the only pattern that brought up the large browns.

In addition to large sculpins other streamers which work well in the spring here are Pearl Marauders, Silver Outcast Streamers, Black Strymphs and Olive-Black Woolly Buggers.

An excellent tactic for early in the season on the Bullpasture is to start at Williamsville and fish up through the "Beaver Falls" with large nymphs such as the Casual Dress and Bitch Creek Nymph both in size 8. The large stones on the stream bottom here hold great numbers of giant stonefly nymphs and the brown trout feed actively upon them and thus respond well to these big artificials.

The campground at the head of the Gorge on the Bullpasture River is a striking area to pitch a tent and start fishing.

If one is quite industrious and willing to put in a very long day it is possible to fish all the way up through the gorge and come out at the upper end. However, there is a tendency to rush by productive water when fishing at this pace. A better ploy is to start at Williamsville and fish upstream at a reasonable pace, then hike back down at the end of the day. An alternate tactic is to park at the campground at the top of the gorge, hike down the canyon about a mile then turn and fish back upstream to the campground. If you find the stream too high to cross easily in the spring there is a footbridge across the stream at the lower end of the campground which puts you on the east side of the stream where you'll have a lot of water to yourself.

Throughout April and May the aquatic insect hatches are very good and one can play the "match-the-hatch" game with dry flies. Or, you can go to a big high-floating dry like a Coachman Trude or Dark Humpy and just cover the water. This latter tactic is best in the fast runs and the edges of heavily broken water.

During summer the large spring at the campground and many smaller springs throughout the gorge keep the Bullpasture cool enough to provide good surface action. My favorite summer flies under these conditions are Ed Shenk's Cricket size 14, Murray's Flying Beetle size 16 and Black McMurray Ants size 16, 18 and 20, all fish on a 9-foot 6X leader.

The Bullpasture River is readily accessible from Route 678 at Williamsville and on upstream for about five miles.

Big browns thrive well in the deep, fast cuts in the remote stretches of the Bullpasture River.

FACILITIES	
BED & BREAKFAST:	**CAMPGROUNDS:**
Fort Lewis Lodge	**Warm Springs Ranger District**
HCR 3 Box 21A	Route 2 Box 30
Millboro, VA 24460	Hot Springs, VA 24445
Phone: (540) 925-2314	Phone: (540) 839-2521
Inn at Gristmill Squire	**Bullpasture State Campground**
P.O. Box 359	4 miles north of Williamsville on
Warm Springs, VA 24484	Route 678
Phone: (540) 839-2231	
MOTEL:	
Highland Inn	
P.O. Box 40	
Main Street	
Monterey, VA 24465	
Phone: (540) 468-2143	

Chapter 18
Jackson River

If you enjoy fishing large trout streams, the Hidden Valley of the Jackson will show you one of the best in Virginia.

When I started fishing the Jackson River over twenty years ago we were evaluating its potential for special regulations to protect its fine trout population. The U.S. Forest Service, Virginia's Department of Game and Inland Fisheries and several conservation organizations all pooled their studies, evaluations and thoughts, and today's fine fishing is a result of their efforts.

The Jackson drains a very long, broad valley and thus is subject to a strong run off in the spring which can often last until April. Since the biological studies in this part of the stream show a large minnow population I like to fish the deep pools with streamers early in the season. If I use a floating line my most consistent tactic is what I call "swinging a streamer." I position myself right beside the deepest part of the pool and cast up-and-across stream at about a 45-degree angle. I allow the streamer to sink to the stream bottom, then I extend the fly rod up and out over the stream while simultaneously stripping in the slack with

The Jackson River is one of the Old Dominion's finest large trout streams.

A delicate rise form along the bank of the Jackson River during the summer is a sure sign of a surface feeder. He could be taking ants falling off the shrubs.

my line hand. By swinging the fly rod in an arc at the same rate at which the streamer is drifting, I have a tight line on my fly which enables me to detect the trout's strike instantly. This technique helps me set the hook quickly thus I miss few takes.

If I am using a sinking-tip fly line I cast across the currents and slightly downstream and use a very slow stripping action to crawl the streamer through the deep pools.

Effective streamers for the Jackson River include Olive Strymphs, White Marabou Muddlers and Black Woolly Buggers all in sizes 8 and 10.

Good aquatic insect hatches start on the Jackson in April with the Quill Gordon representing the first large concentration of sizable mayflies. The duns start emerging about 1 p.m. and continue for the rest of the day with the spinners coming back to the stream to mate and lay their eggs about an hour before dusk.

Some anglers like to just cover all of the likely looking feeding stations with a Mr. Rapidan dry fly or a Quill Gordon dry fly all afternoon whether they spot rising trout or not. Others prefer to wait until dusk when the concentration of both duns and spinners is more likely to have many trout feeding on the surface.

The variety and hatch sequence of the aquatic insects on the Jackson is much the same as is found in the Blue Ridge Mountains in the central part of the state. However, I've often found the hatches on the Jackson starting from ten to fifteen days later in the season. These mayflies in their order of hatching are Quill Gordon, Blue Quill, March Brown, Gray Fox, Light Cahill and Sulphur. See the chapter on the Shenandoah National Park for the hatch charts showing the hatching times and matching artificial dry flies and nymphs (Page 35).

Summer is the favorite time of many anglers for fishing the Jackson River. Admittedly the stream is much lower at this time, and the trout become extremely wary. However, in the heavily shaded area upstream from Muddy Run one can often find the trout sipping-in a variety of small terrestrial insects. After you become familiar with the stream you'll know the areas in which these summer surface feeders locate, for in addition to the shade they will seek out the coolest areas. When I first started fishing here I relied strongly upon detecting the numerous underwater springs by feeling the cool water on my legs as I waded up the stream. Once alerted in this way, I would carefully observe the stream surface for the delicate rise-forms created by the trout sipping-in tiny insects.

My favorite and most productive tactic at this time is to put a size 20 Black McMurray on a 9-foot 6X leader and go one-on-one with rising trout.

The Hidden Valley area of the Jackson River covers about three miles of river and requires hiking to get into some of the best fishing. There is good access at the upstream end by taking Route 623 west off Route 220 north of the town of Warm Springs. The downstream access to Hidden Valley is very popular and here you'll find the National Forest Campground and the Warwick House Mansion. This is accessible by taking Route 621 north off Route 39 west of Warm Springs to Route 615 which leads you to the stream.

FACILITIES

BED & BREAKFAST:
Meadow Lane Lodge
HCR01 Box 110
Warm Springs, VA 24484
Phone: (540) 839-5959

Hidden Valley Bed & Breakfast
The Warwickton Mansion
P.O. Box 53
Warm Springs, VA 24484
Phone: (540) 839-3178

MOTEL:
Roseloe Motel
Rt. 220 North
Hot Springs, VA 24445
Phone: (540) 839-5373

CAMPGROUND:
Warm Springs Ranger District
Rt. 2 Box 30
Hot Springs, VA 24445
Phone: (540) 839-2521
(Request information on the Hidden Valley Campground)

The rich springs and cool feeder streams that enter the Jackson River keep the stream temperature cool for the trout during the summer.

Chapter 19
Back Creek

Back Creek in Bath County is a fine tailwater stream lying in the beautiful remote Allegheny Highlands in the western part of Virginia. Drawing its cool water from the Virginia Power Company's Bath County Pump Storage Station Reservoir, it provides good fishing for brown and rainbow trout.

Many anglers return frequently to this stream to stalk some of the large carryover browns that they come to know on a first-name basis. I'm especially attracted to this stream by the tough, consistent surface feeders it holds.

Early in the season the flow is usually quite strong and the popular tactics are fishing the deep pools and undercut banks with streamers such as the Black Strymph, Spuddler and Olive Woolly Buggers all in size 8 and 10.

By April hatches of Blue Quills and Quill Gordons bring the trout to the surface. Several weeks later the hatches proceed from the March Browns to the Gray Fox and finally the Light Cahills, all assuring excellent dry-fly fishing, especially the last two hours in the evenings. My favorite flies for these hatches are the Blue Quill dry size 16, the Gray Fox dry size 14 and the

A big brown trout closely examines one of Ed Shenk's Crickets on Back Creek.

Light Cahill dry size 16. I use the Mr. Rapidan dry fly during Quill Gordon and March Brown hatch because it floats very well, matches the naturals and the trout take it readily.

I especially like this stream when the flow drops back in late spring and early summer. Almost every long flat pool in the part of the stream which parallels Virginia Power Company's

The cool release from the dam on Back Creek provides a great habitat for its brown trout.

One can almost always find feeding trout in the "bridge pool" on Back Creek.

recreation area will provide trout rising to sip-in terrestrial insects. I remember one day when we estimated that the Bridge Pool had about a dozen trout all rising on separate feeding stations. These trout are almost always very wary so it is wise to approach them very slowly and stay low—even going to your hands and knees if they are in the shallows along the west side of the stream. Two of my most consistent flies for this action are the McMurray Ants in sizes 16, 18 and 20 and Crowe Beetles in sizes 16 and 18, all fished on 6X leaders. True, this is a very demanding game, but once mastered it is extremely gratifying.

The lower section of Back Creek around Blowing Springs Campground and below is higher gradient than the upper section. There are a fair number of deep runs here in which one can do well in the spring by fishing nymphs such as the Cranefly Larva and Casual Dress on fast sinking-tip lines. Many anglers enjoy the solitude they find by hiking downstream and fishing the Back Creek Gorge. This is beautiful remote country so take your camera to record the abundance of wildlife and wildflowers here.

The best fishing on this stream is during the spring and fall since the stream temperatures are best at this time of year.

The upper section of Back Creek is accessible from Haul Road Bridge on Route 600 below the Virginia Power Company Recreation Area, from the recreation area campground and from the Beaver Run Bridge on Route 600 at the upper end of the recreation area.

The lower portion of Back Creek is accessible from Route 39 in the area of Blowing Springs Campground. There is a section around the town of Mountain Grove which is not open to fishing, but there is plenty of excellent water in both the upper and lower sections of the stream.

ACCOMMODATIONS

CAMPGROUNDS:
Warm Springs Ranger District
Route 2 Box 30
Hot Springs, VA 24445
Phone: (540) 839-2521
(Ask for information on the
Blowing Springs Campground)

**Bath County Pump Storage Station
Recreation Area**
Route 600 North of Mountain Grove

MOTELS:
Roseloe Motel
Rt. 220 North
Hot Springs, VA 24445
Phone: (540) 839-5373

Bed & Breakfast:
Inn at Gristmill Square
P.O. Box 359
Warm Springs, VA 24484
Phone: (540) 839-2231

Fort Lewis Lodge
HCR 3 Box 21A
Millboro, VA 24460
Phone: (540) 925-2314

Chapter 20
South Fork of Piney River

The South Fork of Piney River is a very special stream for the fly angler. It contains deep pools, powerful runs and gentle riffles all of which are filled with a broad variety of aquatic insects. Blend this with its wild brook trout that have spent centuries adapting their living and feeding habits to these natural stream conditions and you have wonderful fishing...once you learn to play their game.

For example, one can often find good hatches of Quill Gordon mayflies in late March here with the brookies feeding well on the nymphs in the deep pools as you would expect. However, unlike this hatch on many streams where the spinners come back quite late in the day to mate and deposit their eggs, you can see these Quill Gordon spinners in their mayfly dances and touching down to deposit their eggs into the stream as early as 3 p.m. Obviously this prompts the trout to feed on the surface and gives us great dry-fly fishing.

The first time I encountered this the stream was fairly high and the water was in the mid forties. I was fishing a high gradient part of the upper canyon with a size 12 weighted Quill Gordon Nymph. Since I was picking up a few brookies from

The South Fork of Piney River is a beautiful stream to fish in the fall; the trout usually feed well on the surface and the foliage is magnificent.

The wild brook trout in the South Fork of Piney River are highly revered by anglers for their striking beauty.

the deep pools my thoughts became set on what I was doing and even the occasional rise I saw was discounted as the action of a foolish young dink playing with the tiny Early Dark Stonefly drys. It wasn't until I paused below the tail of one particularly long pool that I realized there were a number of larger trout rising in the flat water at the tail of the pool.

Almost simultaneously the sun upstream over the ridge of the mountain back-lit the Quill Gordon spinners touching down on the water to lay their eggs. The spent spinners that were falling dead on the stream were prompting the trout to feed upon them. I switched over to a size 14 Mr. Rapidan dry fly which is a perfect match for this mayfly and started picking up several trout in almost every pool.

This really made a strong impression on me in that the best trout fishing often comes by being observant of the trouts' feeding habits, the insects and the character of the stream and then adapting one's tactics to these aspects.

In fact the South Fork of Piney River could be considered an excellent "teaching stream" as we reflect upon the above points because of the varying nature of this stream.

The flow in the stream is much greater in the lower area than in the head of the stream so if you feel you are being overpowered in the bottom of the stream just head upstream until you find the level you like best.

The gradient of this stream also varies tremendously over its whole length and one can make great use of this to improve his fishing. One later summer day we spotted a number of trout feeding in the lower flat stretch of the stream but we spooked many of them before we could get close enough to fish to them even though we were approaching them on our hands and knees. The obvious solution was to head upstream into the steep section of the stream where we could conceal our approach below the large boulders. Not only did this enable us to approach each pool without scaring the trout but from our hiding positions we were able to watch individual trout feeding. This let us go one-on-one with specific trout which many anglers feel is one of the most exciting forms of trout fishing.

This stream can get very low late in the summer if we've had a dry season so many anglers prefer fishing it in the spring and early summer.

There are numerous beautiful areas to camp along the stream if you would like to stay here and fish for several days.

There is a section of privately owned land along the stream so treat this with respect and do not camp or fish on private land without the specific landowner's permission.

Shoe Creek is a fine feeder stream that enters this drainage in the lower section from the north above Alhambra. The lower part of Shoe Creek is in private land but the road and stream lead into National Forest land where there is good access and fishing. The further you fish up Shoe Creek the steeper the gradient becomes, producing deeper pools and better fishing.

Shoe Creek has one of the best Sulphur mayfly hatches I've found on a mountain stream in Virginia. The peak of this hatch varies from year to year, but keep an eye out for these delicate little flies any time you are on the stream between the second week in May and early June. The last two hours of daylight will usually provide the best action because you will find a concentration of both duns and spinners on the water at this time. My favorite fly for this hatch is Shenk's Sulfur Dry in sizes 16 and 18. I use these to fish to rising trout and to just cover the water when I do not see rising trout.

Shoe Creek can get very low during the summer, but by using a very cautious approach, a 6X leader and size 16, 18 and 20 beetles and ants you can still get good fishing.

The South Fork of Piney River is located northeast of the city of Buena Vista on the east side of the Blue Ridge Parkway. From Buena Vista take Route 60 east about twenty miles to Route 778 (Lowesville Road) turn left (north) and follow Route 778 to Lowesville. At Lowesville turn left (north) on Route 666 and follow this to Jacks Hill where you turn north (left) on Route 827. Route 827 becomes Forest Service Route 63 which parallels the stream to the top of the mountain. To reach Shoe Creek take Route 745 off Route 827 at Alhambra, cross the stream and follow this into the National Forest land.

FACILITIES

MOTELS:
Budget In
617 West 29th St.
Buena Vista, VA 24416
Phone: (540) 261-2156

Buena Vista Motel
407 East 29th St.
Buena Vista, VA 24416
Phone: (540) 261-2138

BED & BREAKFAST:
The Orchard House
c/o Boxerwood Gardens
963 Ross Rd.
Lexington, VA 24450
Phone: (540) 463-2697

Applewood Inn
P.O. Box 1348
Lexington, VA 24450
Phone: (540) 463-1962 or
1-800-463-1902

CAMPGROUND:
Glen Maury Park
10th Street
Buena Vista, VA 24416
Phone: 1-800-555-8845
Closes in the beginning of November

G. W. NATIONAL FOREST:
Pedlar Ranger District
2424 Magnolia Ave.
Buena Vista, VA 24416
Phone: (540) 261-8856

On Shoe Creek one can often achieve a natural drift by bridging the cast over boulders.

Chapter 21
Pedlar River (Lower)

If you enjoy fishing beautiful high-gradient mountain trout streams in rugged country then the Lower Pedlar River is definitely a stream you should try.

Lying on the east side of the Blue Ridge Mountains and west of the village of Amherst the Lower Pedlar River flows through one of the most beautiful canyons in Virginia. Both upstream and downstream from the Lynchburg Reservoir the gorges provide oxygen-rich water for the trout and it helps produce exceptionally good populations of aquatic insects and minnows.

During the spring one can take many trout both above and below the impressive Panther Falls on giant stonefly nymph patterns such as the Brooks Dark Stonefly Nymph in size 8 and the Casual Dress in size 10. The giant stonefly nymphs live in the heavy water around the largest boulders and this is where I concentrate my nymph fishing. Two of my most productive areas are the deep cuts and the heavy water immediately below the strongest riffles.

By fishing these two areas upstream with a dead-drifting technique I can run my nymphs right along the stream bottom where the trout feed in the full spring streams.

The large deep pools give us good springtime fishing with minnow imitations such as the Black Strymph size 10 and Shenk's Black Sculpin size 8. As long as the stream level is moderately high one can fish downstream with these streamers, effectively swimming them along the stream bottom in all the deep pools and pockets. Once the stream starts dropping, which is usually in April, the streamers are still effective but in order to prevent spooking the trout it is best to wade and fish upstream.

By the middle of April there are usually good hatches of Quill Gordon, Blue Quill and March Brown mayflies and one can often do well with dry flies which match these naturals.

In May, hatches of Light Cahill mayflies and Little Yellow Stoneflies bring the trout to the surface and tapering down to a 5X leader and fishing these patterns in size 16 is very effective.

During the summer the Lower Pedlar River can get very low, but due to the remote nature of much of the stream one can hike into the less fished sections of the gorge and find very good fishing. The thick tree canopy over the stream holds great numbers of ants and beetles and the trout feed very heavily upon them all summer. Patterns such as the Crowe Beetle and the Murray's Flying Beetle in sizes 14 and 16 and the Mr. Rapidan Ant in sizes 16, 18 and 20 all fished on a 6X leader are very productive during the summer.

The gorge on the Lower Pedlar River holds many beautiful small waterfalls that provide great fishing.

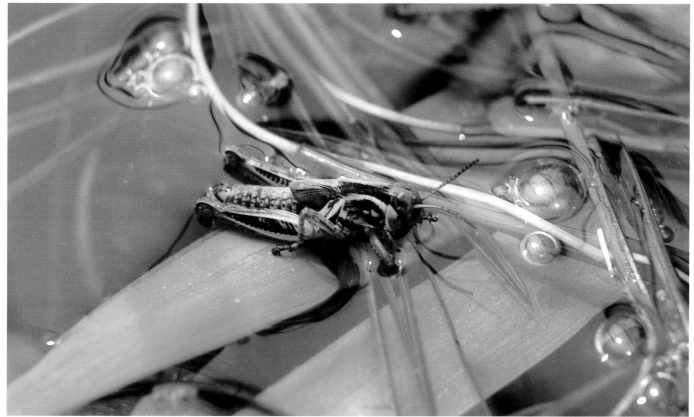

Late in the summer the trout in the Lower Pedlar River often feed heavily upon grasshoppers, drifting a size 14 Dave's Hopper against the banks will take many fish.

Little Irish Creek drains from Coleman Mountain on the west to enter Lower Pedlar River just downstream of the Lynchburg Reservoir. This is a beautiful little stream and is very popular in the spring when it carries a good water level.

The Appalachian Trail crosses the Lower Pedlar River in the area of Little Irish Creek. This provides excellent hiking coming down from the Blue Ridge Parkway on the west crossing the stream below the reservoir then turning north up Brown Mountain.

The National Forest has done an excellent job in providing access to Lower Pedlar River. Downstream of the reservoir along Route 39 they have constructed three large parking areas with good access roads that lead toward the stream. Short hikes are required down to the stream, but the trails are well marked and well maintained. Upstream of the reservoir along Route 315 on the west side of the stream Forest Service Routes 315A and 315C provide good access to the stream with large parking areas and backcountry camping.

The Lower Pedlar River lies about five miles east of the city of Buena Vista on the east side of the Blue Ridge Parkway. Route 60 crosses the stream and there is good access by taking Forest Service Route 39 to the south from Route 60 on the east side of the stream or by taking Forest Service Route 315 south which is on the west side of the stream.

As the Lower Pedlar River begins dropping one can take many nice trout by using a cautious approach.

FACILITIES

MOTELS:

Budget Inn
617 West 29th St.
Buena Vista, VA 24416
Phone: (540) 261-2156

Buena Vista Motel
407 East 29th St.
Buena Vista, VA 24416
Phone: (540) 261-2138

BED & BREAKFAST:

The Orchard House
c/o Boxerwood Gardens
963 Ross Rd.
Lexington, VA 24450
Phone: (540) 463-2697

Applewood Inn
P.O. Box 1348
Lexington, VA 24450
Phone: (540) 463-1962 or 1-800-463-1902

Campground:

Glen Maury Park
10th Street
Buena Vista, VA 24416
Phone: 1-800-555-8845
Closes in beginning of November

G. W. National Forest
Pedlar Ranger District
2424 Magnolia Ave.
Buena Vista, VA 24416
Phone: (540) 261-8856

Chapter 22
Buffalo Creek

Buffalo Creek just south of Lexington is one of Virginia's finest spring creeks.

Originating from the cool North and South branches of Buffalo Creek and picking up the input of many rich springs throughout its course, the Buffalo is assured of cool water throughout the season. I've never recorded a water temperature here above the mid-sixties even in the hottest part of the summer. This ideal temperature and the influence on the acidity of the rich limestone through the springs and along the stream create an ideal habitat for both trout and aquatic insects.

This stream attracts different anglers for different reasons.

For example, some folks hear the reports of the five- and six-pound trout that are caught here and envision taking their largest trout. Others, like a close personal friend, want to match their skills against the selectively feeding brown trout. Both of these goals are possible on this stream, but its fish are very challenging. However, its rewards are quite gratifying.

Since there are fishable water temperatures all season, the Buffalo lets us fish our way through the season, exploring the options.

During the winter the meadows can be covered with snow and the ice crunches under your feet, but the trout are willing to feed. In fact, they often feed on the surface. On overcast days both *Beatis* and *Pseudocloeon* mayflies will bring the trout to the surface. Drifting a size 18 or 20 Parachute Mr. Rapidan over these fish on a 6X leader can give you great action. When the trout are working on these hatches they are not easy to fool. They are drag conscious and very wary, but the thrill one experiences by fooling several of these wise trout is most exhilarating.

At Left: Buffalo Creek, one of Virginia's best spring creeks, has many springs throughout its length that cool it well during the summer.

Below: The meadows along Buffalo Creek hold great numbers of grasshoppers and crickets and the trout take our matching patterns very well.

Late winter and early spring rains and melting snow often cause a slight discoloration in the water. This is the time I like to go "big-fish hunting" with streamers like Shenk's Black Sculpin and the Black Strymph. By searching out the deeply undercut banks and deep pockets you can land some large trout. However, there are no guarantees. Such was the day I decided that I would fish only big streamers all day even if I was getting skunked. From the first undercut bank a two-pound brown swung out and took my Strymph. As I gently released him back into the stream I confidently thought, "good choice of tactics—this will be a banner day." After six hours of fishing my fingers were numb from the cold, I was covered with a mixture of mud and ice and I had not gotten another strike. My thoughts now changed to the realization that, "maybe I had caught the only dumb trout in the stream."

From late March through June there are excellent mayfly and caddisfly hatches. These are basically the same insects and they emerge at the same time as those in the Shenandoah National Park so you can refer to that chapter for the emergence times and matching fly patterns (page 35).

My favorite time on the Buffalo is in the summer. Admittedly, the trout are exceedingly wary in the low, clear water, and I've put down rising trout great distances away while trying to crawl into a casting position. However, this one-on-one game is very exciting. The lower part of this stream has a thick tree canopy which is a constant supply of beetles and ants which the trout take readily. I match these with Crowe Beetles and McMurray Ants. The upper part of the stream flows through more open meadows where the trout see many crickets and grasshoppers. I match these with Shenk's Crickets and Shenk's Letort Hoppers.

The numerous springs that flow into the upper meadows of this stream provide a special bonus to the trout and great action to us. The limestone nature of these springs promotes great concentrations of cress bugs and shrimp and the trout feed heavily upon them. I watch closely for trout rooting out these bugs on the stream bottom and in the aquatic grass. Since these trout will seldom rise to a dry fly when they are locked onto these bugs I use a size 16 wet Cress Bug and cast it about two feet upstream of the trout. I watch the trout closely as the current delivers my fly to him and I strike when I see him move on it.

This terrestrial and cress bug game continues into the fall. By November we start seeing the *Baetis* and *Pseudocloeon* again. So from November on through the winter we're back into our dry-fly game when these hatches are on, we're searching the deep undercuts with streamers and we're always on the look out around the springs for cress bug feeders.

Basically, there is always some trout fishing on Buffalo Creek.

Buffalo Creek is south of Lexington and can be reached by taking Route 251 off Route 11 to Route 612. Take Route 612 left (south). Route 612 parallels the stream and there are numerous parking areas along the stream. There is a fish sanctuary in the lower section of this stream and a block of private land in the upper section where fishing is not allowed. These are clearly marked on the map you get with your free permit. Each angler must have this permit which is issued at no charge by the Virginia Game Department. To obtain this map and permit send your request with a self addressed, stamped envelope to the Virginia Department of Game and Inland Fisheries, Fisheries Division, P.O. Box 996, Verona, VA 24482. A regular Virginia fishing license is also required.

FACILITIES	

Bed & Breakfast:
Maple Hall
  3111 Lee Highway
  Lexington, VA 24450
  Phone: (540) 463-2044
 	
McCampbell Inn
  11 North Main St.
  Lexington, VA 24450
  Phone: (540) 463-2044
	MOTELS:
	Hampton Inn
	  401 E. Nelson St.
	  Lexington, VA 24450
	  Phone: (540) 463-2223
	
	CAMPGROUND:
	The Campground at Natural Bridge
	  Route 782
	  Natural Bridge Station, VA 24579
	  Open from March 15-Dec. 15
	  Phone: (540) 291-2727

By gently releasing the trout back into the stream one helps provide for good future fishing for others.

Chapter 23
North Creek

North Creek is one of the finest trout streams in the Glenwood Ranger District of the Jefferson National Forest. The upper section contains a good population of naturally reproducing trout which are protected by special regulations while the lower portion of the stream is stocked regularly when there is a good stream level. This lower segment of North Creek is in the standard management program with the regular Virginia trout streams.

The North Creek Campground is the general point of reference for anglers on this stream. From the campground upstream you begin catching a fair number of beautiful wild rainbows, then the closer you get to the end of the road the more brook trout you pick up. From the parking area at the end of Forest Service Route 59 on upstream you catch more brookies than rainbows.

At this parking area Cornelius Creek enters North Creek from the southwest. This stream carries only about one half of the water volume of North Creek and it has a good population of wild trout.

This physical drainage stream setup presents what I consider to be one of the most valuable mountain trout situations an angler can ask for. That is, you have three different water levels from which to choose.

If, for example, you hit the stream in March and much to your amazement there is still snow lying in the shaded hollows which is slowly melting raising the water level in the main stream higher than you like. All you have to do to find a more manageable water level is to fish above the junction of North Creek and Cornelius Creek. If you pick the North Creek fork and you still have too much water simply swing over and fish Cornelius Creek.

We can also make good use of this stream setup if we encounter low water in the summer. Under these circumstances we fish the water downstream of the two above branches. In fact, a little further downstream small feeder streams come in from Bryant Ridge on the west and Wildcat Mountain on the east that can help the stream flow. However, I must caution you that in the summers when there is little rain North Creek gets very low.

The rainbows do well above the campground on North Creek.

The good hatches of aquatic insects start on this stream in late March and early April as the water temperature gets above forty degrees. These are the same hatches which occur in the Shenandoah National Park so you can check that chapter on page 35 for their sequence and matching artificial drys and nymphs. One slight exception is that there is a significantly larger caddisfly population on North Creek so one may do well here by devoting more time to fishing Troth's Elk Hair Caddis in sizes 14, 16, 18 in both brown and olive.

The magnificent two-hundred-foot-high Apple Orchard Falls lies two miles up North Creek from the end of Route 59 and is well worth seeing. There is a well-maintained trail to the falls and on up to the Appalachian Trail and to the Sunset Fields Overlook on the Blue Ridge Parkway. This has drawn nationwide attention and the trail is now designated as the "Apple Orchard National Recreation Trail".

This trail provides good stream access to North Creek as does the Cornelius Creek Trail to that stream. In fact, there is a seeded wildlife strip that joins the two trails high in the mountain forming a five-hour loop trail if you would like to see both drainages.

North Creek lies east of the town of Buchanan on the west side of the Blue Ridge Parkway, and can be reached by taking Route 614 at exit 168 off I-81. About one half mile past the village of Arcadia take Route 59 to the left. This road goes to the campground and on up the parking area at the junction of North Creek and Cornelius Creek. You can also access the extreme headwater of North Creek from the Sunset Fields Overlook on the Blue Ridge Parkway. Parker Gap Road (Route 812) and Apple Tree Road (Route 3034) come off the top of the mountain here, but these roads may be closed periodically if conditions are not favorable.

ACCOMMODATIONS

BED & BREAKFAST:

The Berkeley House
64 Old Hollow Rd.
Buchanan, VA 24066
Phone: (540) 254-2548

Braford Cottage B&B
P.O. Box 1
19 Clay Brick Lane
Natural Bridge Station, VA 24579
Phone: (540) 291-2217

MOTELS:

Burger's Country Inn
305 Rices Hill Rd.
Natural Bridge, VA 24578
Phone: (540) 291-2464

Budget Inn
4331 S. Lee Highway
Natural Bridge, VA 24578
Phone: (540) 291-2896

CAMPGROUND:

Glenwood Ranger District
Highway 130, P.O. Box 10
Natural Bridge Station, VA 24579
Phone: (540) 291-2188

Yogi Bear's Jellystone Park
1164 Middle Creek Rd.
Buchanan, VA 24066
Phone: (540) 254-2176

The upper reaches of North Creek carry a good brook trout population that provides good dry-fly fishing in the fall.

Chapter 24
Little Stony Creek

Little Stony Creek west of Blacksburg is my favorite stream in the western part of the state.

Most of it from the National Forest Cascade Parking Area upstream is high gradient with every type cover you could ask for in a freestone mountains stream. There are many deep pools which provide the trout excellent protection even in the lowest water conditions. There are thousands of pockets, each holding several trout that are willing to take a fly, and there are many fast runs that help hide our approach as we stalk the trout. This is all crowned with a beautiful sixty-foot waterfalls about three miles upstream.

The lower portion of this stream holds more rainbows than brook trout. About a mile upstream I seem to pick up about equal numbers of rainbows and brookies. Then about two miles upstream there are a series of shoots and mini-waterfalls which the rainbows apparently can't navigate and the brookies take over. Above the high waterfalls there are only brook trout. About one fourth of a mile above the falls one encounters private land that is not open to fishing.

Lying further south than the trout streams in the Shenandoah National Park one can expect the trout here to start feeding a little earlier in the season. My stream notes indicate that 40 degrees Fahrenheit water temperature is the turn-on point for the brookies, and the rainbows seem to need just a little warmer water to start feeding aggressively. The water temperatures usually reach this point in March. Frequently at this time the stream carries extra water from melting snow and spring rains. This puts us in a dilemma, for most mountain trout fishermen prefer to fish dry flies. However, rather than getting skunked we'll go to nymphs and streamers.

There are many sculpin minnows in this stream so a logical fly to fish in the deep pools if the stream is high is Shenk's Black Sculpin in size 10. I find that I take more trout on streamers in these small streams by fishing and wading upstream rather than the conventional tactic of fishing them downstream. I believe there are two reasons for this marked success. First one is much less likely to scare the trout by approaching them from below and, second, this enables us to run our flies deeper which is where the trout are holding in the cool, full streams.

Nymphs are also very effective here in the early spring. Patterns such as the Mr. Rapidan Bead Head and the Fox Squirrel Bead Head Nymphs both in sizes 10, 12 and 14 will seldom let you down in Little Stony Creek. Since the stream varies greatly in depth from pool to pool early in the year the one constant for success is to run your flies along the stream bottom. The easiest way to achieve this is with the upstream dead drifting tactic, using a 9-foot 4X knotted leader with one Scientific Anglers Indicator about two feet above the nymph and a second indicator two feet above the first one. Wading upstream and casting up and slightly across stream and watching these indicators for the strike will give you many trout.

By late March the aquatic insects begin to hatch and as the water drops and warms the trout rise well to drys. The specific insects, their hatching sequence and the matching fly patterns are shown on page 35, in the charts in the chapter on the Shenandoah National Park. The peak emergence of specific insects on Little Stony Creek may average a week or so earlier than in the Shenandoah National Park because the water here warms earlier. This will vary from year to year so one should always be observant if the desire is to match the hatch.

From June into late fall, terrestrial insects are the main fare for these trout so one can seldom go wrong with dry Crickets, Beetles and Ants as long as the water temperature stays above 40 degrees Fahrenheit. After this you may do well with streamers and nymphs again.

Little Stony Creek is the type stream that one becomes closer to the more he fishes it. For with its great carrying capacity and favorable water temperatures one can come to know a specific trout on a specific feeding station and match wits with him many times throughout the season.

Little Stony Creek can be reached by turning north on Route 623 at the town of Pembroke which is on Route 460. Follow Route 623 to the end of the road and park in the National Forest parking area.

If you would like to fish for smallmouth bass while you are in this area the New River flows right by Pembroke (page 29) and there is access just upstream. See Chapter 5 on the New River for tactics and further access.

FACILITIES	
BED & BREAKFAST: **River Bend Farm** 225 Zells Mill Rd. Newport, VA 24128 Phone: (540) 544-7849	**Carden's Motel** 141 Virginia Ave. Rich Creek, VA 24147 Phone: (540) 726-2362
Linda Lorraine's of Pearisburg 1409 Cabot Dr. Pearisburg, VA 24134 Phone: (540) 921-2069	**CAMPGROUNDS:** **Blacksburg Ranger District** **National Forest** 110 South Park Dr. Blacksburg, VA 24060 Phone: (540) 552-4641
MOTELS: **Mountain Lake Resort** 115 Hotel Circle Mountain Lake, VA 24136 Phone: (540) 626-7121	**Dixie Caverns** 5753 West Main St. Salem, VA 24153 Phone: (540) 380-2085

Little Stony Creek produces some of the most beautiful brook trout one can find as this striking male shows.

The large pools in the lower reaches of Little Stony Creek hold many rainbows and brook trout that rise well to dry flies.

Chapter 25
Big Stony Creek

Big Stony Creek west of Pembroke is a very popular trout stream for it provides excellent road access throughout its whole length and it is heavily stocked by the Virginia Department of Game and Inland Fisheries during good flow periods. It is almost two streams in one for the lower portion is high gradient with many deep pools and fast runs while the upper section around the village of Interior is much flatter.

During March and April a popular way to fish the lower section is with streamers and nymphs. Use special care to search out the deep card table-size pockets with your flies since these all hold nice trout which are often missed by anglers who devote their time to the large pools.

This lower section of Big Stony Creek holds a large population of chub, dace and darter minnows. In fact, one of the endangered darter minnow is found here.

Excellent streamer imitations to use here are the Black Strymph, White Marabou Muddler and Shenk's Black Sculpin all in sizes 8 and 10.

Big Stony Creek gives great early season fishing for browns and rainbows in its lower reaches.

In the spring the lower portion of this stream is large enough to use conventional down and across stream tactics which let you swim your streamer through all of the best holding water. However, in the deepest pools and fastest runs you may need a sinking-tip line or mini-sinking head in order to reach the protected areas along the stream bottom where the trout are holding.

General impressionistic nymphs such as the Casual Dress and Hare's Ear both in sizes 8, 10 and 12 are good here in the spring.

If you prefer dry-fly fishing early in the season you will find good action in the upstream section where the lower gradient provides shallower pools and more gentle flows.

The majority of trout here are stocked, and they seldom fine tune their appetites to the point that we must precisely match the emerging insects. General attractor patterns such as Coachman Trudes and Irresistible Wulffs both in size 12 and 14 fished on 4X leaders will usually do the job.

During the early part of the summer one can do well with terrestrial patterns here. But this stream drops drastically during the summer and the trout become vary wary.

There are many fine stream improvements put in the upper section of Big Stony by Trout Unlimited, the Boy Scouts and others that help provide cover for the trout during the summer. There is even excellent wheel chair access here. One effective

The rainbows grow beautiful and very strong in the fast runs on Big Stony Creek.

summer tactic is to sneak through the rhododendron and spot rising trout around these stream improvements, then crawl into a hidden casting position and go one on one with the feeding trout.

October can provide good fishing if there are rains to bring the stream level up.

To reach Big Stony Creek take Route 635 north off Route 460 two miles west of Pembroke. Route 635 follows the whole stream.

Giant stonefly nymphs thrive well in the high-gradient stretches of Big Stony Creek.

FACILITIES

BED & BREAKFAST:
River Bend Farm
225 Zells Mill Rd.
Newport, VA 24128
Phone: (540) 544-7849

Linda Lorraine's of Pearisburg
1409 Cabot Dr.
Pearisburg, VA 24134
Phone: (540) 921-2069

MOTELS:
Mountain Lake Resort
115 Hotel Circle
Mountain Lake, VA 24136
Phone: (540) 626-7121

Carden's Motel
141 Virginia Ave.
Rich Creek, VA 24147
Phone: (540) 726-2362

CAMPGROUNDS:
Blacksburg Ranger District National Forest
110 South Park Dr.
Blacksburg, VA 24060
Phone: (540) 552-4641

Dixie Caverns
5753 West Main St.
Salem, VA 24153
Phone: (540) 380-2085

Chapter 26
Big Tumbling Creek

Big Tumbling Creek is one of Virginia's largest mountain trout streams and lies in one of the most beautiful settings in the state. It is nestled in the towering ridges of the Virginia Department of Game and Inland Fisheries 25,000-acre Clinch Mountain Wildlife Management Area.

There is an excellent cool-water source from the 300-acre Laurel Bed Lake located in the head of Big Tumbling Creek and from several small feeder streams. This affords ideal conditions for the trout throughout the summer.

Big Tumbling Creek is managed as a fee fishing area wherein the angler pays a modest daily fee to fish the stream and this fee goes to raise the trout which are stocked regularly into the stream. This helps assure a high degree of success for the anglers. The popularity of this system is quickly recognized by the realization that approximately 13,000 daily fishing permits are sold annually to anglers from all over the East Coast and that over seventy percent of the anglers interviewed recently on the stream felt their fishing had been good to excellent.

In addition to the stocked rainbows and browns there is good rainbow trout reproduction throughout the stream. Both species carry over well from one season to the next thus providing a good supply of tough, wary trout which can challenge the most accomplished anglers. These carry-over trout are often found in the deep cuts and deep fast pockets that can be more difficult to read and to fish than the picturesque pools.

Good fishing usually begins on this stream in early April. Since the stream can be either high or cold or both at this time, many anglers rely on streamers such as the Black Strymph, the Olive Strymph and the Black Woolly Buggers all in size 10. The trout here quickly become accustomed to feeding on the abundant minnow population and they take these streamers readily. The deeper and slower you fish these flies the more trout you usually catch.

The high-gradient portion of this stream is loaded with large stoneflies so early in the season you take many trout on

Big Tumbling Creek flows through one of the most beautiful parts of the state and due to a special management system holds a large trout population.

the Casual Dress Nymph and Murray's Hellgrammite both in size 10. Fish these upstream dead drift in the deep cuts and pockets mentioned earlier and you can pick up some quite large trout.

From the middle of April until early June there are good hatches of aquatic insects and you can do well by fishing either to rising trout or just covering the best looking feeding stations. The Quill Gordons and the March Browns are two of the best mayfly hatches here and the Mr. Rapidan is an excellent match for these so you can hardly go wrong fishing the Mr. Rapidan Dry Fly in size 14 and the Mr. Rapidan Bead Head Nymph in size 12 throughout April and May.

Other effective early season dry flies include the Royal Wulff, Coachman Trude, Dark Humpy and Parachute Adams all in sizes 14 and 16.

By June the Little Yellow Stoneflies and Sulphurs represent the major aquatic hatches and are well worth matching by the artificial flies by these names in sizes 16. One can start making impressive catches by June on terrestrial patterns such as Shenk's Cricket, McMurray Ants, Crowe Beetles and Dave's Hoppers. I like to carry a broad assortment of sizes in terrestrials, from size 10 in the Hoppers and Crickets down to size 22 in the Ants.

Throughout the entire summer and into late fall one can expect to get good action with terrestrials.

Once the water temperature drops below forty degrees late in the fall the best catches usually come to the same nymphs and streamers which did well early in the spring.

This is an excellent area for a family vacation, for in addition to the fishing there are excellent facilities for camping, horseback riding, hiking, nature photography and wildlife viewing.

Camping for the angler and his family is a very rewarding experience in the Clinch Mountain Wildlife Management Area that cradles Big Tumbling Creek.

If you are interested in history the town of Saltville which is right beside the Clinch Mountain Wildlife Management Area is fascinating. The rich salt deposits here started attracting animals after the ice age and controlled archeological digs here by Dr. Jerry McDonald of Radford University and others have discovered the remains of animals from 15,000 years ago. This rich salt deposit earned it the name of the "salt capital of the Confederacy" and prompted several battles for the area. The Museum of the Middle Appalachians at Saltville is extremely well done and well worth seeing.

Big Tumbling Creek is easy to reach by taking exit 35 off I-81 at Chilhowie and following Route 107 to Saltville. In Saltville, turn left onto Route 91 (1/4 mile); then right onto Route 634; bear left onto Route 613 and proceed 3 1/2 miles; then right onto Route 747. There are numerous signs along the route directing you to the "Clinch Mountain Wildlife Management Area."

Even during the winter one can find good trout fishing on Big Tumbling Creek.

FACILITIES

MOTELS:

Empire Motel
887 Empire Drive
I-81, Exit 19
Abingdon, VA 24210
Phone: (540) 628-7131

Hampton Inn
340 Commerce Dr.
I-81, Exit 17
Abingdon, VA 24210
Phone: (540) 619-4600

BED & BREAKFAST:

The Love House
210 E. Valley St.
Abingdon, VA 24210
Phone: (540) 623-1281

Silversmith Inn
102 E. Main St.
Abingdon, VA 24210
Phone: (540) 676-3924

CAMPGROUND:

Clinch Mountain Wildlife Management Area
VA Commission of Game and Inland Fisheries
P.O. Box 1110
Richmond, VA 23230
Phone: (804) 257-1000

Hungry Mother State Park
2854 Park Blvd.
Marion, VA 24354
Phone: (540) 783-3422

Chapter 27
Big Cedar Creek

Big Cedar Creek north of the town of Lebanon in Russell County is one of the most striking streams in Virginia.

The state has placed the lower part of Big Cedar Creek and the Clinch River, into which it flows, in their Scenic River Classification and justifiably so. The waterfalls and pinnacle rock areas here are worth the trip just to see them.

In a conservation project between The Nature Conservancy and the citizens of Russel County this point of land between Big Cedar Creek and the Clinch River has been set aside as the "Pinnacle Natural Area Preserve." This is managed by the Virginia Department of Conservation and Recreation to provide habitat for many rare plants and animals. In fact one rare mussel which is found in only two rivers in the world is here.

The lower portion of this road is a little rough but if one uses care you can drive all the way to the parking area below the falls.

This is a good area to begin your fishing because if you want privacy you can start here and fish downstream for about a half mile to where this stream empties into the Clinch River. This is a remote, rugged part of the stream which hold a good trout population in the spring. And, if you're so inclined, as my son Jeff often is, you can fish the Clinch River where Big Cedar flows in for smallmouth bass.

This lower part of Big Cedar Creek is big water and in the spring nymphs and streamers are both very productive fished down and across stream.

I like to go in below the falls and cover the lower part of this large holding pool with drys such as a Royal Wulff or Mr. Rapidan in sizes 14. First I cast to any rising trout I can spot, then I cover all of the likely looking feeding stations, especially along the banks and around the big back run on the right side below the falls. Next I like to fish tight up under the falls with nymphs like the Mr. Rapidan Bead Head and the Casual Dress both in sizes 10 and 12.

The trout in Big Cedar Creek feast on the abundance of minnows in the stream and grow rapidly.

Big Cedar Creek is a fine spring and early summer trout stream in the Pinnacle Natural Area Preserve in southwest Virginia.

Since the road above the falls swings high on the ridge away from the stream one can find good action and often privacy by continuing to fish upstream above the falls. This section is also accessible by coming in from above where the road swings back to the stream. You can enter the upper end and fish downstream with streamers for several hours and come out below the falls.

There is good water both above and below where the road crosses the stream, but being more accessible, this gets much more pressure.

From mid April until June there is good fishing throughout the stream with dry flies. These trout are usually not selective so good floating, highly visible patterns such as the Light Humpy, Royal Wulff and Parachute Adams in sizes 14 and 16 are popular flies.

The stream gets quite warm late in the summer so you will probably do better to wait until fall for the better action.

While you are in this area you may like to fish the Clinch River for smallmouth bass. Nash Ford is just west of Big Cedar Creek and this is one of my favorite areas on the Clinch River. See Chapter 6, page 30 on the Clinch River for the access areas and tactics on that river.

Big Cedar Creek can be reached from the town of Lebanon by taking Route 82 west for about one mile, turn right (north) onto Route 640, follow this about four miles then take a left (west) on Route 721 and follow this to the end of the road.

FACILITIES

BED & BREAKFAST:
Summerfield Inn
101 W. Valley St.
Abingdon, VA 24210
Phone: (540) 628-5905

Inn on Town Creek
445 E. Valley St.
Abingdon, VA 24210
Phone: (540) 628-4560

MOTELS:
Alpine Motor Lodge
I-81 Exit 19
Abingdon, VA 24210
Phone: (540) 628-3178

Empire Motor Lodge
I-81 Exit 19
887 Empire Drive
Abingdon, VA 24210
Phone: (540) 628-7131

OTHER INFORMATION:
Clinch Ranger District, U.S. Forest Service
9416 Darden Drive
Wise, VA 24293
Phone: (540) 328-2931

The falls on Big Cedar Creek provide oxygen-rich water to the trout prompting good fishing.

Chapter 28
South Fork Holston River

This stream is almost two different waters with greatly different types of fishing within one drainage.

The stream within the boundary of the Buller Fish Cultural Station is presently managed as catch-and-release water. There are some very large trout here but due to the pressure they receive they are very difficult to catch.

Two of the best tactics to use here take advantage of the extremes of the scale in fly sizes. If you see rising trout here they are often coming to midges so crawl into a concealed casting position, taper down to a 7X leader, knot on a size 22 Black Midge and go one on one with your trout. The second ploy takes advantage of the great minnow population in this stream upon which the trout feed regularly in low light levels. Here

The abundance of small natural insects on the South Fork of the Holston River prompt the trout to feed selectively, requiring us to match the naturals for consistent success.

The South Fork of the Holston River has many rich springs feeding the area above the Appalachian Trail footbridge.

you would go in early in the morning or late in the evening and carefully cover all of the good looking water with streamers which mimic these minnows. Shenk's White Streamer, Cream Strymphs, and Black Marauders all in sizes 6, 8, and 10 are excellent big-fish minnow imitations.

There is some nice typical freestone water above this point which produces good fishing to rising trout in April when the hatches of Quill Gordons and March Browns are at their peaks. If you have time try to fish until dusk when the spinners return because you'll see many more feeding trout.

Now for the second type fishing—which is by far my favorite on this stream.

The upper reaches of this stream in the vicinity of where the Appalachian Trail crosses it takes on a spring creek nature. The water here is very rich, coming from many springs for the next several miles upstream. This has a positive influence on the stream's alkalinity which promotes very good insect populations and trout growth. It also cools the summer stream temperatures. In fact, I've never gotten a water temperature above the mid-60s here even in the summer.

Some of the most rewarding trout fishing here takes place in the summer. There are pretty good hatches of Tricos and *Baetis*, but I especially enjoy the terrestrial fishing. There is a great canopy of trees and shrubs here that produce a steady flow of landborn insects for the trout. If you stand quietly in the stream, hiding behind some low sweeping tree limbs, it is not at all unusual to spot four or five trout sipping food from the surface fifty feet upstream.

My favorite way to fish this upper area in the summer is to wade slowly up the stream and look for surface feeders, then gently ease up to within casting distance. Since I am practically working up through a tunnel of tree limbs the casting position needs to be very carefully selected. I must be able to get there without spooking the trout which means I may have to climb over tree limbs or crawl under overhanging shrubs. And the casting spot must allow me to get the cast off some way without scaring the trout.

The rainbows in the South Fork of the Holston River are very strong and beautifully colored.

I realize this sounds like a lot of work just to be able to drift a fly over a rising rainbow, but the gratification which comes from putting it all together and fooling him is magnificent.

I use many Hoppers, Crickets, Beetles, Ants and Jassids here. My most consistent patterns are the Mr. Rapidan Ant in sizes 16, 18, and 20, Shenk's Cricket sizes 14 and 16 and Murray's Flying Beetle sizes 14 and 16.

Keep in mind that those same springs which cool these upper reaches in the summer also produce warmer water here during the winter than a true freestone stream would have.

These trout can be taken during the winter on the same streamers mentioned earlier, but now I would use them in sizes 10 and 12. Also keep an eye out for the *Baetis* which can hatch any time during the winter, especially on heavily overcast days.

If I spot risers here in the winter I go to a Baetis Parachute in sizes 18 and 22 or a Mr. Rapidan Parachute in sizes 18 and 20. I fish all of these on a 9-foot. 6X or 7X leader.

Since the canopy is so tight and the angling so demanding in this upper section I like a 7 1/2- or 8-foot rod which handles a number 2 or 3 line.

This stream lies south of Marion. The lower area at the Buller Fish Cultural station can be reached on Route 650 off Routes 658 and 657 south of Route 11. The upper section lies west of Sugar Grove along Route 670.

FACILITIES

BED & BREAKFAST:
Fox Hill Inn
8568 Troutdale Highway
Troutdale, VA 24378
Phone: (800) 874-3313

Tranquility Lodging
John Collier
P.O. Box 138
1324 Ripshin Rd.
Troutdale, VA 24378
Phone: (540) 677-3638

MOTELS:
Wilson's Cabins
3077 Park Blvd.
Marion, VA 24354
Phone: (540) 783-6792

Budget Host Inn
435 S. Main St.
Marion, VA 24354
Phone: (540) 783-8511

CAMPGROUNDS:
Houndshell Campground
12749 Flatridge Rd.
Troutdale, VA 24378
Phone: (540) 655-4639

Hungry Mother State Park
2854 Park Blvd.
Marion, VA 24354
Phone: (540) 783-3422

Chapter 29
Whitetop Laurel

Whitetop Laurel is definitely one of the finest trout streams in Virginia. It has an outstanding population of wild rainbows and enough large browns to keep you on your toes. However, there is much more to this area than just its trout which causes one to pause in appreciation to the Creator. The towering ridges and vast wilderness areas quickly give one deep feelings of sincere gratification for the privilege of just being here.

The Mount Rogers National Recreation Area, which cradles this stream, covers 119,000 acres of National Forest land around Mount Rogers, which at 5,729 feet is the highest point in Virginia. The Crest Zone at over 4,000 feet elevation covers 5,000 acres of magnificent spruce-fir forest. There are three Congressionally designated wilderness areas containing a total of over 10,000 acres ranging in elevation from 3,240 feet to 5,729 feet. The Mount Rogers Scenic Byway traverses 55 miles offering views of the National Recreation Area and open rural countryside. There are nine developed campgrounds and over 300 miles of maintained trails, including 60 miles of the Appalachian Trail and 18 miles of Virginia Creeper Trail.

The Virginia Creeper Trail parallels some of the finest water in Whitetop Laurel, and gives excellent access to anglers. The 33-mile Virginia Creeper Trail connects Abingdon, Virginia with the Virginia-Carolina border a mile east of Whitetop Station, Virginia. This trail was originally used by Native Americans, then settlers such as Daniel Boone and finally became a railroad in 1905. The railroad was used in transporting iron ore, lumber and passengers until 1977. Its "Virginia Creeper" name came from the slow pace set by early steam locomotives as they struggled up the steep grade.

Lying in the extreme southern part of Virginia this stream provides good fishing earlier and later in the season than many other streams.

It is quite common to see several species of Early Dark Stoneflies in sizes 18 and 20 sitting on the snow banks along the stream in February. However, one has a much better chance of digging the trout out with nymphs such as a size 10 Hare's Ear or a size 12 Red Squirrel than by drifting small dry stone-fly patterns.

By mid March one can expect good surface action with good hatches of Blue Quill Mayflies. These are closely followed with March Browns then the Gray Fox, then the Light Cahills. Throughout March and April the trout are seldom selective and a naturally drifting Dark Humpy, Mr. Rapidan and Parachute Adams in sizes 12, 14 and 16 will usually do the job.

An assortment of terrestrial fly patterns helps meet the whims of the trout on Whitetop Laurel during the summer.

The brown trout become wise and wary as they get large on Whitetop Laurel requiring the utmost of the angler's skills.

As the stream drops in May the Sulphurs start emerging and one becomes aware of the need for more finesse to fool some of the larger trout in the heavily fished areas. A size 16 Sulphur dry fly on a 5X leader will often fool trout that pass up the larger patterns.

Throughout the summer these Sulphurs, small Elk Hair Caddis and Parachute Adams do well in matching the aquatic insects while McMurray Ants, Flying Beetles and Shenk's Crickets are excellent as searching patterns. In many of the deep pools in the high-gradient parts of the stream one may take a fish or two off the lip of the pool but they may refuse to raise in the deepest part of the pool. This is your cue to run a nymph such as a Bead Head Pheasant Tail or Bead Head Prince through the deepest runs before you. There are very large brown trout in the deep cuts in the shade of the old trestles that seem oblivious to one's perfectly presented dry fly that will fall to the nymphs drifted down on their levels.

There is good water on Whitetop Laurel from Damascus to beyond Konnarock. Popular areas include that part of the stream which parallels Route 58 starting about 4 miles east of Damascus. The Virginia Creeper Trail provides good access here. I especially like the section of special regulation water in Taylors Valley. To reach this area take Route 58 east of Damascus about one half mile and turn south (right) on Route 91. Follow this about two miles and turn north (left) on Route 725 and follow this up to the gate beside the stream. This puts you at the downstream end of the special regulation water which reaches up to the mouth of Green Cove Creek which is

an excellent small feeder stream. You can access the mouth of Green Cove Creek and fish either stream by coming in Route 728 south off Route 58 about two miles west of Konnarock.

There are National Forest Service information facilities at Damascus and at Green Cove on Route 600. A nice Forest Service campground is located on Straight Branch on Route 837. More information is available at:

Mount Rogers
National Recreation Area
3714 Highway 16
Marion VA 24354
Phone: (540) 783-5196

FACILITIES

MOTELS:

Best Western Motel
1424 N. Main St.
Marion, VA 24354
Phone: (540) 783-3193

Econo Lodge
1424 North Main St.
Marion, VA 24354
Phone: (540) 783-6031

CAMPING:

Grayson Highland State Park
829 Grayson Highland Lane
Mouth of Wilson, VA 24363
Phone: (540) 579-7092

BED & BREAKFAST:

Fox Hill Inn
8568 Troutdale Highway
Troutdale, VA 24378
Phone: 1-800-874-3313

Tranquility Lodging
John Collier
P.O. Box 138
1324 Ripshin Rd.
Troutdale, VA 24378
Phone: (540) 677-3638

Chapter 30
Big Wilson Creek

I've fished mountain freestone trout streams all over the country and Big Wilson holds its own with the best of them.

Part of its appeal is its large population of wild rainbows and brook trout that rise so well to a dry fly.

Additionally, it is one of the most beautiful streams I've ever seen. The gradient in the upper reaches is very steep, and it is laced with boulders the size of a car. This provides excellent cover for the trout, for even in periods of low water there is adequate depth for protection of the trout.

Drawing its origin from the cool springs to the east of Mount Rogers in rugged terrain which is almost a mile high, the trout are assured of cool water all summer.

When you stand at the bottom of Big Wilson Creek and look up the mountain you cannot help but be impressed with its grandeur. It seems to flow out from between two gigantic columns which beckon you. Actually, these are Bearpen Ridge on the east and Big Spring Ridge on the west. Further up Wilbur Ridge on the northwest leads you up to Mount Rodgers.

This area is so striking that it is managed in a way that all future generations of anglers will be able to enjoy it. The stream is bordered on the northeast by the Little Wilson Creek Wilderness Area on the west by the Grayson Highland State Park, and on the north by National Forest land.

The wild brook trout in Big Wilson Creek are draped in colorful beauty much like their surroundings.

The fishing is truly outstanding. The action becomes very dependable by the middle of March with the hatches the same as shown in the chapter on the Shenandoah National Park. Use the hatch charts on page 35 so you will know which insects will be appearing when and the fly patterns which match them. However, it seems to me the hatches on Big Wilson begin about two weeks earlier than the same insects in the Park.

Additionally, this stream often has good hatches of Green Drake mayflies in April and May so be willing to stay on the stream until dusk to take advantage of the spinner fall of coffin flies. It is often so dark when these spinners return to the stream that the trout are not selective in their feeding, so a size 12 Irresistible Wulff usually does the job.

During the early part of the summer Little Yellow Stoneflies

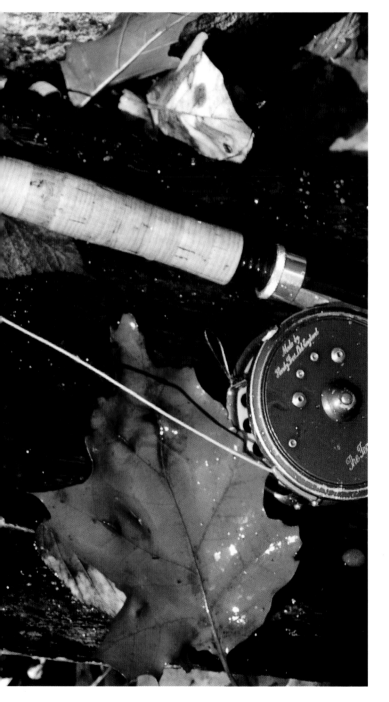

The upper reaches of Big Wilson Creek hold many deep pools guarded by its huge boulders.

in a size 16 as well as terrestrials are productive, and from July until November terrestrials such as Shenk's Cricket, Parachute Black Ants and Murray's Flying Beetles are excellent.

In the upper reaches of the stream where the huge boulders occur there are some surprisingly deep pools for a stream this small. Even in the summer when you are taking several trout from each pool on drys it is wise to search out some of these depths with a heavy nymph. Such a ploy often produces some of the largest trout.

Little Wilson enters this stream from the east in this steep area and is an excellent trout stream in its own right. This carries only about one third of the water of Big Wilson so in the spring if Big Wilson is a little high just walk on up the mountain and fish Little Wilson. I often use this trick and find outstanding fishing.

Big Wilson Creek can be reached by taking Route 817 northwest off Route 58 about a half mile east of the village of Mill Creek which is located a little over twenty miles east of Damascus. Route 817 parallels Big Wilson Creek. I like to drive to the end of the road and fish upstream from there.

FACILITIES

BED & BREAKFAST:
Fox Hill Inn
  8568 Troutdale Hwy..
  Troutdale, VA 24378
  Phone: 800-874-3313

Davis-Bourne Inn
  119 Journey's End
  Independence, VA 24348
  Phone: (540) 773-9384

MOTELS:
Evergreen Lodge
  139 Evergreen Lane
  Independence, VA 24348
  Phone: (540) 773-2859

Cabin On The Ridge
  548 York Ridge Rd.
  Mouth of Wilson, VA 24363
  Phone: (540) 579-4452

CAMPING:
Grayson Highland State Park
  829 Grayson Highland Lane
  Mouth of Wilson, VA 24363
  Phone: (540) 579-7092

Shady Shack Campground
  2872 Jefferson Highway
  Mouth of Wilson, VA 24363
  Phone: (540) 579-2193

Chapter 31
Rock Castle Creek

Rock Castle Creek is a beautiful mountain freestone draining the eastern side of Blue Ridge Parkway in the Grassy Knoll and Rocky Knob area south and west of Route 8. The lower section of the stream, downstream from Route 8, is stocked with brown trout and rainbows and flows through a gentle, flat area with easy stream access and easy fishing.

The most exciting and beautiful part of Rock Castle Creek is in the Rocky Knob Recreation Area above the end of the road where Little Rock Castle Creek comes in from the north.

This area contains an excellent population of rainbows which rise well to size 14 and 16 hatch matching drys in the spring such as Mr. Rapidans and March Browns. I do well here throughout the summer with size 16 Crickets and Beetles fished on 6X. As you fish further and further up the mountain you begin picking up more brook trout. These increase in number the further up you fish.

This is one of those streams that one can do well on in the spring if the streams in the valley floor are high and carrying too much water for good fishing. By hiking high up into the mountain you get above many of the wet weather hollows which can reduce your stream flow considerably within a few miles giving you excellent fishing. Also the brook trout seem to feed more aggressively in colder water than the rainbows and this in itself can put the odds in your favor in the upper reaches of Rock Castle Creek.

The stream volume holds up fairly well in this stream during the summer, but a cautious approach is often needed to consistently take the best fish. At this time of the year I like to pause well below each pool and examine them very carefully before moving in to make my first cast.

In many cases this minute or two study of the pool will reveal a rising trout or if there is good light I can often spot a few trout on feeding stations even if I don't see them rise. Once I locate the trout I go in at a low angle to prevent scaring them. If the pool is fairly flat I'll even go to my hands and knees as I move into a secure casting position. This one-on-one contest with a trout you've located in one of these headwater areas is

The reward for hiking high up into Rock Castle Creek is the wild brook trout whose ivory-edged fins and scarlet spots make one very appreciative to the Creator.

Rock Castle Creek, fed by the cool headwater hollows high in the Blue Ridge Mountains, offers good trout fishing all summer.

one of the most rewarding forms of angling. If you do it all correctly and get a natural drift you'll get your trout. Botch any part of the game and he'll show you he's dealing the cards.

Rock Castle Creek is crossed by Route 8 about three miles northwest of the town of Woolwine, in Patrick County. The stocked section can be reached by taking Route 678 north off Route 8. The section containing the population of wild rainbows and brook trout can be reached by taking the road south where Route 8 crosses the stream and drive to the end of the road.

The Little Yellow Stoneflies are on the upper reaches of Rock Castle Creek from May until July and the trout feed heavily upon them.

FACILITIES

BED & BREAKFAST:
Dutchies View Bed & Breakfast
10448 Woolwine HWY..
Woolwine, VA 24185
Phone: (540) 930-3701

Mountain Rose Inn
1787 Charity HWY..
Woolwine, VA 24185
Phone: (540) 930-1057

MOTELS:
The Virginian Motel
P.O. Box 1326
Stuart, VA 24171
Phone: (540) 694-4244

Tuggles Gap Motel
3351 Parkway Lane South
Floyd, VA 24091
Phone: (540) 745-3402

CAMPGROUND:
Fairy Stone State Park
967 Fairy Stone Lake Drive
Stuart, VA 24171
Phone: (540) 930-2424 (Cabins also available)

Deer Run Campground
P.O. Box 6
Woolwine, VA 24185
Phone: (540) 930-1235

Chapter 32
Smith River

Serious anglers hold the Smith River at Bassett in such high esteem because it contains an excellent population of wild brown trout. In fact the Virginia Department of Game and Inland Fisheries has estimated that over 50 percent of all of the natural reproducing brown trout in Virginia live in the Smith River.

Initially this great trout reproduction seemed too good to be true because the stream is a tailwater fishery below Philpot Dam which is used to generate electricity. When they are generating power a tremendous amount of water charges down the Smith River. Some way, however, the browns have adapted to these regular surges of water to reproduce and adapt and grow well in the river. In fact, Hank Norton who knows the stream very well feels that it is presently carrying its maximum capacity of browns perfectly. He attributes this to the ideal cover and feeding areas the stream affords.

Harry Steeves, who is an expert on the aquatic insects in this river, hits squarely on the attraction this stream holds for many of us when he speaks admiringly of the willingness of its browns to feed regularly on the surface when there are good hatches.

Gently returning the trout to the Smith River
helps assure good future angling.

The elusive banks of fog dancing across the Smith River seem
indicative of the finicky feeding habits of her trout.

Some of the greatest hatches are quite small insects which one may find difficult to believe when you see the water volume which rips through the stream channel when they are generating at Philpot Dam. However, like the brown trout the insects have adapted extremely well.

The Smith River has produced browns over 18 pounds and a good number have topped 10 pounds. But as a friend recently stated when I told him of the size of some of the fish the Smith,..."They didn't get that big by eating bugs." This is exactly true. The shad and other food fish which come through the dam when they are generating form the trout-stream equivalent of "feeding time at the zoo."

If you're after an exceptionally large brown your best bet is to hit it on the "falling water" after the generating has stopped because it takes several hours for the stream to drop back to the normal low flow. Raking a size 4 Shenk's White Streamer or Cream Strymph across the stream on a 7-weight rod just might give you the largest brown you've ever caught. But I must caution that you could easily try this on one hundred consecutive trips and never get your monster. "It's a long time between drinks".

A better ploy, and one which has been very good for me, for much faster action is to fish the falling water with large nymphs and drys before it drops to the low flow.

One of my best days came with fishing a size 6 Bitch Creek Nymph upstream dead drift in the fast runs while the stream was a long way from its low flow. In fact, I had to be very careful where I waded in order not to get into trouble. Then as the stream dropped a little more I took Hank Norton's suggestion and fished the runs with a size 14 Royal Wulff. The fishing was great until the river got down to its low level, then the browns got tough.

However, this low level with its challenging trout selectively feeding on small natural insects is what attracts most of us to the Smith. It is not that we relish having the stream whip us to where we come away being skunked. But those trout that insist on lying there right in front of you, steadily sipping something so small from the surface that you have trouble identifying it in your small insect net as you seine the stream's surface, are something special. Mastering this challenge and fooling some of these wise browns on a 7X leader with a size 24 fly is very gratifying.

Now I must caution you, this quest can be addicting and one gets the feeling that "with just the right fly" I could fool most of those trout. I shouldn't tell you this story lest you feel I'm a nut, but since it is true here goes. Just as I was about to stop fishing on the last day of a three-day trip to the Smith one August I slipped and fell in just deep enough to get the two fly boxes in the bottom pockets of my vest wet and all of the flies became soaked. This of course can ruin the small midge drys. Since my friend was planning to drive the three-hour trip back home I felt this would be a good chance to string my wet midges across the car dash where the sun would dry them before we got home. This was fine but my mistake came when, out of boredom, I decided to count them as I placed them back in the fly boxes when they became dry. Much to my surprise and embarrassment I counted over nine hundred midges as I returned them to their specific compartments. And, I had still come up against many browns that were too smart for me! Tough trout!

Some of the most dependable surface action on the Smith is in May and early June when the Sulphur hatch is on. These flies start emerging here in the morning when the hatch commences and get later in the day until by June they are on at dusk. I like to pick out specific fish and go one on one with them. My favorite dry patterns are Shenk's Sulphur, Harrop's Gray/Yellow No Hackle and Harrop's Hair Wing No Hackle Sulphur Dun all in sizes 16 and 18.

During the summer I fish a lot of Beetles and Ants from size 14 down to 22 as well as Chironomid Midge patterns in olive, cream, tan, gray and black in sizes 20 to 26.

From fall throughout the winter the midges are still on and there are excellent little *Baetis* hatches.

The trout can be very selective on the *Baetis* and seem to examine our flies with a magnifying glass. Consequently I use many different patterns. The ones I have my best success with are Gray Olive No Hackle (Baetis Dun) in sizes 20 and 24, the Parachute Baetis in size 22 and the Mr. Rapidan Parachute Dry in size 20.

There is good brown trout water from Philpot Dam downstream to the village of Koehler. The popular area is the special regulation water from Towne Creek off Route 674 for three miles down to the Route 666 bridge in Basset. However, I've had excellent fishing right in the town of Bassett.

For information on the generating schedule call the Philpot Dam at: (540) 629-2432

FACILITIES

BED & BREAKFAST:
Maple Springs Inn
263 Ridgewood Lane
Patrick Springs, VA 24133
Phone: (540) 629-2954

MOTELS:
Hampton Inn
50 Hampton Dr., US 220 Business
Martinsville, VA 24112
Phone: (540) 647-4700

Dutch Inn
US Highway 220 North
Collinsville, VA 24078
Phone: (540) 647-3721

CAMPGROUND:
Fairy Stone State Park
967 Fairy Stone Lake Drive
Stuart, VA 24171
Phone: (540) 930-2424
Cabins also available.

Wise brown trout selectively sipping tiny insects from the crystal-clear stream are the magnets
which repeatedly pull anglers back to the Smith River.

Chapter 33
Dan River

The Dan River is a very unusual freestone mountain stream for the Old Dominion for there are two large dams on it which are owned by the city of Danville.

Actually, these dams are the primary reason the Dan is as good as it is because they help stabilize the water level and the water temperatures in the stream.

For example, when these dams catch extra rain and snow run-off in the spring one can find good fishable water levels in the Dan River even when many other streams in the area are too high to fish. Then during periods of low water which can adversely affect the fishing in other close-by mountain streams, the Dan can provide good fishing as this stored water is gradually released.

This same catching-storing-and-releasing of water by the dams can have a positive influence upon the stream's water temperatures which sparks the trouts' feeding and thus our angling action.

It is not at all unusual for the water temperature in the Dan to run significantly warmer in the winter and early spring months than other mountain streams in the area. When you

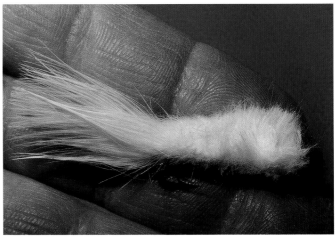

Shenk's White Streamer is very effective in the deep pools and pockets on the Dan River.

During the summer, skillful anglers like to go one-on-one with rising trout on the Dan River.

realize that the trouts' "turn-on" temperature ranges from forty to forty-five degrees it is easy to see that if the Dan River below these dams is running from the mid to the upper forties in late February you can expect the trout to be feeding much more actively and the fishing to be significantly better than on a freestone stream in which the water temperature is in the upper thirties or low forties.

This stabilization of the stream's water temperature may be even more significant to our fishing during the summer when many other streams get warm. Although I've never found water temperatures above seventy degrees in any headwater mountain trout streams, even in the warmest part of the summer, I've definitely noticed a reluctance in the trout to feed actively as this water temperature is approached. It often appears that many of trout are just "holding on" as the water temperature approaches seventy degrees. In the case of the Dan River the trout are not stressed with these warmer water temperatures and thus continue to feed quite well all summer.

There are actually three different parts of the Dan River which you may want to consider fishing.

From the Pinnacles Hydroelectric Powerplant downstream the stream falls into the conventional state regulations and is stocked with trout.

From the Pinnacles Hydroelectric Powerplant upstream to Townes Dam there is about three miles of excellent water with a good population of reproducing brown trout. The further up this section of the stream you fish the better the action is. There is a rough trail along this section of the stream. In order to protect this fine fishery the Virginia Department of Game and Inland Fisheries has placed special angling regulations on it. Be sure to check the regulations before you fish here to make sure you are in compliance.

From Townes Dam the Dan River extends about five miles upstream to Talbot Dam. This section contains an excellent population of reproducing brown and rainbow trout and is also protected by special regulations which may differ from those below Townes Dam so check the regulations before fishing.

The most popular access to the stream between the two dams is by canoe. Take your canoe or small boat by car to the designated parking area at Townes Dam. Cross the lake and head upstream about a mile to a mile and a half to where the

The dams on the Dan River help assure good winter trout fishing.

stream enters the lake. Wade and fish upstream from here. This area can also be accessed by driving to Talbot Dam, parking at the designated area and hiking down the stream and fishing back up. This, however, is very rugged country and most serious anglers choose the former access by canoe.

There are fairly good hatches throughout the stream, but these trout are seldom selective. Effective patterns include the Coachman Trude, Adams Parachute, and Mr. Rapidan drys in sizes 14 to 18. Popular nymphs are the Bead Head Prince and Bead Head Hare's Ear in sizes 10, 12, and 14. There is a good population of Giant Stoneflies in this stream so if you hit a deep pool you suspect of holding a big brown that doesn't want your conventional patterns you may want to try him with a size 8 Brook's Dark Stonefly Nymph. Keep in mind that these big browns did not reach this size by being stupid, so if you know where one lives go in quietly, maybe even on our hands and knees, in order to give yourself an advantage.

The one time these trout can be selective is if there is a concentration of Chironomid Midges on the water. Jeff Handy who knows this stream very well talks quite admiringly of the feeding frenzy which goes on in the lower part of the stream when the trout lock onto these insects. I always start out by trying midge feeders with a size 20, 22 or 24 Black, Gray, or Olive Midge Dry, but if I get refusals on these I grease all but the last three inches of my leader with silicone cream and try them with a size 18 or 20 Bead Head Serendipity or Brassie on 7X.

In order to fish the Dan River a permit is required from the City of Danville and can be obtained at no charge from the Pinnacles Powerhouse or City Utilities Department, Director of Electric Division, Department of Utilities, P.O. Box 3300, 6211 Kibler Valley Rd., Ararat VA 24053. City Phone: (540) 251-5141 and Powerhouse Phone: (540) 251-5141.

Access

To reach the lower portion of this stream go south from the town of Stuart on Route 8 for 4.2 miles to Route 103. Turn right (west) on Route 103. Go to the village of Claudville. Turn right (northwest) on route 773 and follow this 1.4 miles to Route 648. Turn right (northwest) on Route 648 and follow this 6.2 miles to the hydro plant.——To reach the upper part of the Dan River take Route 614 south from the Meadows of Dan. Route 601 turns left to take you to Talbott Reservoir. A little further along Route 614 you can take Route 602 to the left which leads to Townes Reservoir. Park only at the designated parking areas.

FACILITIES	
BED & BREAKFAST: **Spangler's Bed & Breakfast** 1340 Mayberry Church Rd. Meadows of Dan, VA 24120 Phone: (540) 952-2454	**CAMPGROUNDS:** **Meadows of Dan Campground** 2182 Jeb Stuart HWY.. Meadows of Dan, VA 24120 Phone: (540) 952-2292
MOTELS: **Blue Ridge Motel** Rt. 2, Box 12 Meadows of Dan, VA 24120 Phone: (540) 952-2244	**Round Meadows Campground** 10750 Squirrel Bur Rd. Meadows of Dan, VA 24120 Phone: (540) 952-2604
Doe Run Lodge M. P. 189 Blue Ridge Parkway Fancy Gap, VA 24328 Phone: (800) 325-6189	

Chapter 34
Stewart's Creek

Through excellent stream management by the Virginia Commission of Game and Inland Fisheries, Stewart's Creek now holds a wonderful population of aquatic insects and wild trout.

I f you like to catch wild brook trout in mountain streams then Stewart's Creek is for you.

Since brook trout seem to feed more aggressively at lower water temperatures than browns and rainbows, and with this stream lying on Virginia's southern border it is possible to get some great surface action here before it is possible in many of the streams further north.

Often there are good hatches of Quill Gordons and Blue Quills early in March when the water temperature is over forty degrees. In fact, if there happens to be a low water level at this time it may be the best fishing of the season. If, however, the stream is running full and you have water in the low forties you can take plenty of brookies on nymphs like the Quill Gordon, the Mr. Rapidan Bead Head and the Cranefly Larva all in sizes 12 and 14.

From late spring into the summer you can consistently take fish throughout the stream on standard hatch-matching patterns as well as attractor patterns such as Light Humpies and Coachman Trudes in sizes 14 and 16.

I especially like the summer on this stream because for a mountain stream its water level holds up extremely well and the temperature stays below seventy degrees. This prompts the trout to feed regularly. Since the hatches are over, I fish mostly with Shenk's Crickets and Murray's Flying Beetles in sizes 14 and 16 and Black Parachute Ants in sizes 16, 18, and 20.

As you fish further and further up the stream the gradient increases greatly and there are many deep pools cut out below the numerous mini-waterfall. This is ideal habitat for brook trout for it provides them with well-protected holding water and ideal feeding stations.

The beautiful wild brook trout in Stewart's Creek can be very challenging, but once one refines their tactics the fishing is very gratifying.

Stewart's Creek, lying in the southern part of the Old Dominion, becomes warm earlier in the spring than many other streams and offers excellent early season fishing.

In this type water one often finds the largest trout in each pool in the protected "corner feeding stations". These are identified as dinner plate-size miniature back eddies located immediately to the sides of the incoming riffles or falls, and they are almost always right in front of a large boulder which forms the uppermost boundary of the pool. Natural insects which fall or drift into these corners do not last long before "Mr. Big" sips them in as a meal.

With an astonishing degree of consistency, my largest brook trout in Stewart's Creek practically always come to a dry fly drifted naturally in these corners. Whether it is a Mr. Rapidan Dry Fly in March when the Quill Gordon Mayflies are hatching or Shenk's Cricket in the summer when the terrestrials are out, these "corners" seldom let me down. This is what prompts me to refer to them as the primary feeding stations in these pools. Loosely defined, the "primary feeding station" is that area which holds the largest trout in each pool.

There is good fishing here well into December unless winter moves in earlier than normal.

Keep in mind that these trout spawn in late October and November so treat them with respect at this time. Most anglers do not feel comfortable fishing for the brookies while they are on the spawning beds, but there are periods before and after this when the fishing is great. Caution: Be careful not to wade through the spawning beds after the trout have left them. This could easily destroy many eggs and result in the loss of many young trout in the spring.

As we fish Stewart's Creek and enjoy its wild brook trout in this beautiful, rugged country we should be especially appreciative to the Virginia Department of Game and Inland Fisheries who purchased over 1,000 acres here in 1987 and saved this stream from dangerous logging practices which were rapidly taking their toll on these fine wild trout. The establishment of the Stewart's Creek Wildlife Management Area is a real gift to the anglers of this and future generations.

Stewart's Creek lies in the triangle formed by the Blue Ridge Parkway, Route 77 and the Virginia-North Carolina border. The closest village is Lambsburg where you take Route 696 west several miles to Route 795 and follow this to the parking lot at the end of the road on the right of the stream. The trail is on the right side of the stream. About one mile upstream the stream forks and the South Fork to the left is the largest branch.

FACILITIES

BED & BREAKFAST:
Bray's Manor
P.O. Box 385
123 Stag Ln.
Hillsville, VA 24343
Phone: (540) 728-7901

MOTELS:
Best Western Motel
Rt. 1 Box 360
Hillsville, VA 24343
Phone: (540) 728-4136

Doe Run Lodge
M. P. 189 Blue Ridge Parkway
Fancy Gap VA 24328
Phone: 800-325-6189

CAMPGROUND:
R-J Ranch Campground
8736 Double Cabin Rd.
Hillsville VA 24343
Phone: (540) 766-3703

INDEX